Appliqué Workshop

MIX & MATCH 10 TECHNIQUES TO UNLOCK YOUR CREATIVITY

LAUREL ANDERSON

C&T PUBLISHING

Text copyright © 2010 by Laurel Anderson

Artwork copyright © 2010 by C&T Publishing, Inc.

Publisher: Amy Marson

Creative Director: Gailen Runge

Acquisitions Editor: Susanne Woods

Editors: Jake Finch and Lynn Koolish

Technical Editor: Nanette S. Zeller and Carolyn Aune

Copyeditor/Proofreader: Wordfirm Inc.

Cover/Book Designer: Kristen Yenche

Production Coordinators: Zinnia Heinzmann and Jenny Leicester

Production Editor: Julia Cianci

Illustrator: Laurel Anderson

Photography by Christina Carty-Francis and Diane Pedersen of C&T Publishing, Inc., unless otherwise noted.

Published by C&T Publishing, Inc., P.O. Box 1456, Lafayette, CA 94549

Library of Congress Cataloging-in-Publication Data

Anderson, Laurel.

Appliqué workshop : mix & match 10 techniques to unlock your creativity / Laurel Anderson.

  p. cm.

ISBN 978-1-57120-835-4 (soft cover)

1. Appliqué. 2. Quilting. I. Title.

TT779.A583 2010

746.44'5--dc22

                          2009043849

Printed in China

10 9 8 7 6 5 4 3 2 1

Table of Contents

Dedication

This book is dedicated to my mother, Marilyn Wolfkill. She taught me to sew when I was young. She was convinced that everyone wished to admire all of my creative projects. We had a show-and-tell every time she had guests. She was an accomplished clothing maker and a real inspiration. She made her first quilt when she was 67. I am so proud of her.

Laurel Anderson and Marilyn Wolfkill, daughter and mom

Acknowledgments

The journey to a finished book requires the input of many people. There are several who require special thanks. First of all, thanks to Laura Hohlwein, my InDesign instructor, who insisted I submit the first chapters as my class final. Also to Nancy MacDonald who has done through this process with her own book. She helped me anticipate the steps involved in the publishing process. Thanks for the support of my Monday afternoon quilting group: Mary Wilkinson, Wini Fung, Helen Powell, Pat Gossett, Balvina Reed, JoAnna Schwilk, and of course Nancy MacDonald. Thanks also for the encouragement and support of my neighbor, Chris Shores-Hague.

Thanks also to the talent from C&T who patiently worked with me: Jake Finch, Nanette Zeller, Julia Cianci, Gailen Runge, Carolyn Aune, Jenny Leicester, Zinnia Heinzmann, Lynn Koolish, Christina Carty-Francis, Diane Pedersen, and Kristen Yenche.

Thanks to my family for their patience and endurance through this project. They pitched in to help in so many ways.

Introduction: Unlock the Creative Power of Appliqué

Appliqué, with its rounded shapes and free-flowing lines, has always appealed to me. I am not alone in this love; I've noticed when I attend quilt shows that the appliqué quilts seem to consistently win the most Best of Show awards.

I started quilting by sewing squares of fabric together. These basic quilts were made from donated fabric and tied with donated yarn for one of the homeless shelters in my community. The shelter didn't care about the beauty of the quilts. The staff and their clients were delighted with the quilts' warmth and durability.

From squares, I moved on to triangles and then strips for a Log Cabin design. After a few years of stitching geometric designs, I signed up for an appliqué class. My first class covered hand-appliquéd hearts. My second class focused on reverse hand appliqué, circles, and stems. After these hand appliqué classes, I took a class in freezer paper machine appliqué. Classes are a wonderful way to learn! Because I am a visual learner, I learn best when I am shown each step. That's why I've included many illustrations in each chapter of this book. I hope this makes learning the techniques easy for you.

My life is busy. I have three kids, a nursing career, and a parent who needs care. My quilting time is limited, so I use any technique that fits into my busy life. Like many nurses, I find quilting therapeutic. It offers balance to the giving and serving roles of a health-care occupation. We caregivers are used to imagining successful results from the labor of our hands, but in quilting we really have control of the outcome. I can experiment as much as I wish in quilting. A mistake in health care could be deadly, but an ugly quilt is still warm.

For every quilter there will be a favorite technique. This book will help you explore a wide variety of appliqué methods to find your own favorites. Hand appliqué is the oldest method of turned edge appliqué, but there are many other methods that can be used to turn under the edges of your appliqué pieces and stitch them down securely on your project. If you wish to jump ahead and explore the faster methods of raw edge appliqué, turn to page 48.

It is my wish that after working through the appliqué exercises found in this book, you will fall as deeply in love with appliqué as I have. Whatever method or methods you settle upon to make your projects, remember that the goal is to enjoy the process and the results.

Color and Design Principles for Your Appliqué

Value

Before you rush off to the fabric store, we need to talk about value. Everyone with a degree in fine art knows the magic of value. It is more important than color. Value describes how light or dark the color is. Pure white and saturated black are the two extremes, with every color and print falling in between. I have made quilts that included every color in my stash, such as *August Gold*. These quilts are interesting to look at because I used separate areas of light and dark. If you like to make scrappy quilts with no color planning, you must use value to make your quilts dramatic. Turn off your lights and view your fabrics in minimal light. This makes it easier to ignore the colors and just see the value of each fabric.

Most of us buy fabrics in medium-range values. Fabric manufacturers know this and produce mostly medium-value colors. It can be hard to find very light or very dark fabrics. Buy them as often as you can.

All of the areas of interest within your quilt are considered your composition. Within your quilt's composition, high-contrast areas will look closer to the viewer. Low-contrast areas, such as the pastel, blurry background of *Show Off*, will visibly recede. The bold black-and-white prints used for *Mount Diablo* (page 14) seem to demand attention, looking as if they're ready to leap out of the dull, red frame. Try on a pair of glasses that are the wrong prescription for you. Stand back and look at the blurry colors and shapes within your quilt. What areas in your quilt stand out? Are you pleased with the color and value changes? If this blurry image were modern art, would you buy it?

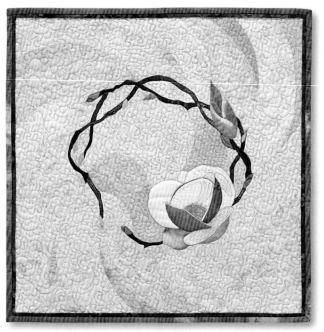

Show Off by Laurel Anderson, 18″ × 18″

Freezer paper machine appliqué. This quilt's pastel background causes the eye to perceive that it's receding into the background.

August Gold by Laurel Anderson, 103″ × 103″

Paper foundation pieced. This quilt used almost every leaf fabric from my stash to highlight the range of colors and values needed.

Temperature

The temperature of a color describes its warmth or coolness. Think of warm as the colors found in fire and cool as colors of water. Warm colors include yellow, orange, red, fuchsia, and purple. Cool colors range from green and blue through violet. Bright, warm colors move visually closer when viewed. In *April*, all of the colors are bright. The cool, cobalt blue background is dramatic, but not as dramatic as the warm red and yellow. This warm/cool contrast gives the flowers added drama.

Saturation

Saturation measures a color's purity. Fully saturated colors are called *vivid*. Colors with undertones of gray, white, or brown are called *muted* or *pastel*. One of my leaf greens is so bright that I have never used it in another quilt. I used just a sliver of it in *April*, and it looks tame in this color-saturated quilt. Remember that color saturation and value are to be compared with the other colors in the quilt. A quilt containing only medium values will be serene. Dull colors next to bright colors will increase the drama of the brights. A quilt made from only brights will look playful and childish. The lightest or darkest fabric will always draw the eye. A quilt design with blacks and whites will look gray if the prints are small or the fabric pieces small. Don't play fair. Give one design area value and color dominance. Also remember that the quilting thread color will be part of the final product. If you match the thread to the fabric color, you'll accentuate the fabric. Or, use a thread color that will blur the colors, as in the background of the quilt *Show Off* (page 6).

April by Laurel Anderson, 18″ × 18″

Freezer paper machine appliqué. The play between the cool, deep cobalt background and the warmth of the flowers adds drama to this quilt.

Composition

As I learned about photography, I was taught to put something high in value contrast at the photo's one-third mark. This catches the attention of the viewer. Note the third mark on *Sunlight* (below) and *April.* (page 7). Where the marks intersect, there is a design element to demand attention.

We've all seen quilts that are so busy visually, you're almost dizzy when you look at them. In every quilt you design, offer your viewers a place to rest the eye. Blank spaces and undecorated spaces are as attention grabbing as the main subject. Pay attention to the shapes created by the blank space. Make the lines within this space draw the eye toward the main subject.

Think about the design principles of similarity and difference. If all of the design elements are the same size and are evenly spaced, the eye sees the quilt as a whole. It is hard to focus on a part of the quilt as a "subject." Many pieced quilts are this way. If many of the parts of the quilt are similar but a few are different, then the viewer is attracted to the areas that are different and will likely stop to look at the quilt closely. The most interesting Baltimore Album quilts have a center medallion or a unique border that is different from the evenly spaced blocks of appliqué.

It Is Good to Be Odd

From the world of jewelry accessorizing comes the advice that odd numbers are much more interesting than even numbers. Try this: Count all of the areas in your quilt that demand attention. Don't count the leaves or flowers that fade into the background. It may help to dim the lights to view the high-contrast areas of the quilt. If you are working with an even number of squares, you might choose to reduce the value contrast of one or three to end up with an odd number of high-contrast subjects.

Texture

Texture refers to the appearance of the quilt surface. Does it look soft, smooth, bumpy, or rough? Texture includes the print within the fabric, the appearance of the piecing, and the stitches of the quilting. Try to combine a variety of textures in your design. You can do this with the design itself by designing areas that are busy and areas that rest the eye. Remember that the quilt stitching will become part of the quilt's texture. Choose fabrics that vary in texture and print size. Select quilting designs and threads that enhance the appeal of the main subject and blur the background.

Sunlight by Laurel Anderson, 61" × 40"

APPLIQUÉ WORKSHOP

Color Wheel

Fabric dyer's color wheel

It's wonderful to work on a quilt when you know the colors you've chosen will be enjoyed for decades to come. Color adds to the drama or the serenity of the image. Even black, white, and gray are colorful enough to provide a visual and emotional impact. There is a tool used by artists called a color wheel, which will help you learn about how colors work. Art supply and paint stores regularly stock them.

The common color combinations are called monochromatic, complementary, analogous, triadic, and quadratic. I'll explain each of these in a moment, but first, a note about color wheels. The artist's color wheel is based on the primary colors of yellow, blue, and red, just as you learned in elementary school. The color wheel for printers and fabric dyers, or the Ives color wheel, is slightly different. Yellow, cyan, and magenta are the primaries for print; and yellow, turquoise, and fuchsia are used for dyeing. Any of these will work well for your quilting.

Online help with color wheel choices can be found at www.colorschemedesigner.com. At www.colormatters.com, you'll find a lot of information about color, including color blindness, the emotional impact of colors, and current color trends.

MONOCHROMATIC

The monochromatic color scheme features one color with lighter and darker versions included. Black, gray, and white may be added. This choice usually results in a sophisticated, serene quilt. Or try all red or purple for a dramatic look.

COMPLEMENTARY

Complements are two colors located directly opposite each other on the color wheel. The danger with using complements comes from working with both colors in pure and saturated hues. Picture a pure clear blue paired with a vibrant, pure orange. Ouch! Our human eyes will see motion where the two colors meet, and this can be exhausting to live with. When experimenting with complements, try, instead, to tone down one of the colors by using it in a darker or paler colored fabric choice. The interest will still be there, but the clash will disappear.

ANALOGOUS

An analogous color arrangement includes up to five colors that are located next to each other on the color wheel. This includes all the pastel and dark versions of the five colors. Analogous color schemes can be delightful to work with! I suggest choosing one color that dominates your design and adding in several others for smaller shots of sparkle.

Autumn Breeze by Laurel Anderson, 40" × 40"

Fusible appliqué. In this quilt, beautiful fall colors are closely related and truly reflect the autumn season.

TRIADIC

This is my personal favorite of all of the color schemes. In it, three colors are used that are equidistant from one another on the color wheel. Red, blue, and yellow are the primary triad. These can look childish if used in saturated hues. Orange, green, and purple are the secondary triad colors. Think of a summer sunset with long purple shadows.

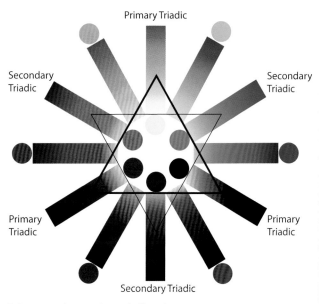

Primary and secondary triadic colors

QUADRATIC

The quadratic color scheme uses two sets of complementary colors together. The colors chosen may be evenly spaced around the color wheel or chosen at random. You may have noticed these color combinations in modern art. This can be a very exciting color scheme if used carefully.

The color wheel is an excellent starting point for understanding color and how we react to it, but it's by no means the only tool at your disposal. *Joen Wolfrom's 3-in-1 Color Tool*, from C&T Publishing, is a great tool for selecting colors. Trust your own instincts as well as those of other designers and artists you admire. For instance, the color wheel model does not tell you that black, white, and red look great together. It won't share with you that beige quilts look like they must be touched. There are so many other ways to create pleasing color palettes. Try each method that interests you, and use your own evaluation for the results.

Tulips Trio by Laurel Anderson, 22″ × 26″

Cut-and-glue appliqué. This quilt is made stunning by dramatic use of red, black, and white.

Focus Fabric

It's easy to choose colors for your quilt's design using a favorite fabric. For those of you just testing your design wings, this is a great place to start. First, choose a print fabric you would like to use as a focus fabric. Next, select fabrics that match all of the colors in this focus print. To create a harmonious quilt, I recommend sticking to the proportions of each color found in the print. So, if the dominant color in the focus fabric is red, then design around larger areas of red. If the focus fabric has small spots of yellow, keep your use of yellow small. Do not be afraid to edit the colors. The quilt *Inherit the Love* on page 76 is based on the focus fabric used in the quilt.

Home Décor

Let your own home inspire you. I often choose fabric colors for my quilt designs from the room in which the finished quilt will hang. If the wall or bed is in a dark area, choose bright or light colors. High contrast between lights and darks will enhance a dark space. On the other hand, a bright, well-lit wall will make a vivid quilt visually scream. Put it in your exercise room for added inspiration to sweat!

Copy Colors in Fine Art and Photographs

Use a favorite photo or painting for inspiration as you would a focus fabric. Copyrights cover images but not color combinations, so choose your colors from the inspiration piece. Copy the quantity of each color used as well.

Here's one of my favorite tricks for gleaning color inspiration. Turn to magazines and tap into the talents of their art directors! The colors used on magazine covers are carefully planned and controlled. Take one to the quilt shop with you and match the colors to fabric. Bridal magazines offer issues featuring bridal flowers. These issues are treasure troves of beautiful color combinations.

Seasons

Let's flash back to the 1980s when everyone was getting their colors done by professional image consultants. A trained consultant helped her client choose the most flattering colors for the client's skin and hair tones, and then showed the client how to apply those colors to clothing choices. Everyone was loosely grouped into color seasons with color samples to match. This same theory will work beautifully in your quilt designs, because the colors in a seasonal group work well together. Play with the four seasons that follow, and consider making your next quilt in the season that looks best on you!

FRESH SPRING

Spring represents colors with yellow undertones: spring green, yellow, peach, purple, and any other colors found in a meadow of wild flowers. Include the colors of the sky and water.

Spring Sigh by Laurel Anderson, 24″ × 21″
Freezer paper appliqué. Spring's colors sing loudly here.

THE COLORS OF SUMMER

Summer's colors tend to go well with soft pinks. Also, look at colors with blue undertones, milk chocolate brown, dove gray, sky blue, lavender, or other colors that remind you of an English cottage.

First Kiss Tulip by Laurel Anderson,
9″ × 22″

Freezer paper appliqué. This lovely tulip takes everything about summer's colors and gives it back to us in a very pretty, fresh way.

EARTHY AUTUMN

In autumn, it's all about greens with brown and gold tints. All the rich reds, oranges, browns, and golds belong to this group. These colors go well with heavily textured fabrics. Animal prints or heavy embellishment coordinate well with autumn color choices.

Iris Wreath Pillow by Laurel Anderson, 18″ × 18″

Freezer paper machine appliqué. A perfect accessory for your bed or couch, this lovely pillow shows off autumn's bounty of rich colors perfectly.

THE DRAMA OF WINTER

Winter represents our power colors, like black and white with fire-engine red or saturated fuchsia. Winter's colors include colors with an undertone of ice blue and gray. Silver lamé or other silver metallic fabrics work in this color season.

Mount Diablo by Laurel Anderson, 18″ × 15″

Freezer paper machine appliqué. The dramatic use of black-and-white fabrics captures the viewer's eye.

International

Research your heritage. Choose quilt colors from the native art of your family's past. Try the earthy colors of African art, or look to the blue and white of Delft china from Holland. How about the colors commonly found in Norwegian hand-knit sweaters? Copy the greens, golds, and reds from a Chinese dragon painting. Photograph a sari from India and use its colors and textures. Choose the fall colors of a Native American basket. Mimic the colors in a Mexican festival or a Middle Eastern tile floor.

Delft ornament

East Indian tapestry

Nepalese scarf

When using a wide variety of colors, remember not to play fair. Choose one color to dominate. Use the others in smaller amounts.

Historical

The history of quilting records the world's history in fabric. The poverty of the war years shows in the well-used shirting prints and tea-dyed, muted colors of the Civil War era. Quilts from the 1850s were often simple in their color combinations. Red, pink, and green are common from that era.

Prints from the 1930s are often childish in their colors. Many quilts from the 1930s were made from flour sacks. Garments were used until completely worn out during the Great Depression, and then they became bedding. The United States was prosperous during the 1950s. The prints made then were often bold and saturated with high-contrasting color.

1850s-style quilt thought to be made by Sarah Goettler or Mabel Griggs

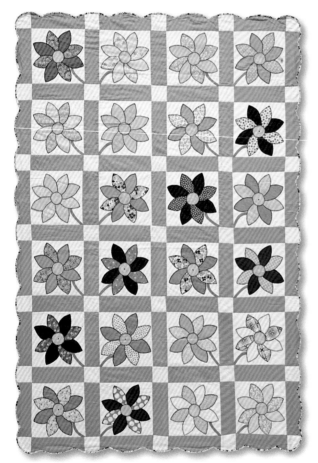

1930s quilt, maker unknown

In the 1960s, quilting was not popular, especially with the younger generation. Macramé was in fashion. The colors associated with that era are fun to use. Tie-dye became popular, along with very large, very bold prints.

In the 1970s, quilting became a fad. With the Bicentennial in 1976, a patriotic-themed quilt competition received enormous attention. Quilting was recognized as an art form with enormous potential for self-expression and political commentary. Polyester double knit was easier to find than cotton fabrics. The cottons available were called calicos. These were small, ditsy prints usually paired with brown.

Using Color in Your Appliqué

Color and design inspiration can be found in many places. When designing your quilt, refer back to the principles discussed in this chapter. Try a new color combination for each new quilt. It's easy to create a beautiful quilt composition with just a little bit of planning. Remember that your favorite colors will provide you with many years of enjoyment. When choosing fabric for the flower patterns in the coming chapters, ignore the colors used in the example. Choose your own favorite colors. In nature, irises bloom in most colors except red. Tulips bloom in most colors except blue. Dogwood trees blossom in white, green, red, and pink. Coneflowers come in most colors except blue, and calla lilies come in many colors including black.

Appliqué Ratings Chart

There are so many different ways to accomplish appliqué that I thought a good place to start opening this stitching world for you would be with an overview of the different techniques, what they require, and how they're accomplished. Of course, I'll be reviewing each of these techniques in-depth in the later chapters, but for now, this should serve as a good primer for sticking your toe into the appliqué waters.

To begin with, all appliqué techniques can be divided into two categories: turned edge appliqué and raw edge appliqué. There are several ways to accomplish each technique using a sewing machine or handwork. With the turned edge techniques, the appliqué piece's edges are turned to the wrong side of the piece, creating a crisp, folded seam along the edge. This technique requires a bit more work, but the results are especially helpful for projects that will see a lot of washing and/or wear, such as bed quilts, because the turned edges prevent fraying. Raw edge techniques are often, but not always, better suited for projects that will not be handled as much, such as wallhangings, and can sometimes provide more intricacy in the designs.

The Appliqué Ratings Chart can be used as a reference to compare options when deciding on which appliqué technique to use for a particular project.

Appliqué Method	Supplies Required*	Best For	Sewing Recommendations	Washing Recommendations	Softness (1 = soft to 5 = firm)	Difficulty (1 = easy to 5 = complex)
Turned Edge Appliqué Using Starch (page 24)	• Freezer paper • Starch	• Gentle shapes and sharp angles	• Machine zigzag, hem stitch, straight stitch, or hand stitch • Stitch edges and remove freezer paper before layering quilt sandwich	• Prewash fabrics (optional) • Finished quilt OK to wash or dry-clean	1	3
Turned Edge Appliqué Using Gluestick (page 29)	• Freezer paper • Washable gluestick	• Any shape including sharp angles and deep curves	• Machine zigzag, hem stitch, straight stitch, or hand stitch • Stitch edges and remove freezer paper before layering quilt sandwich	• Prewash fabrics to avoid bleeding. Soak appliqué to remove glue and freezer paper • Finished quilt OK to wash or dry-clean	1	3
Turned Edge Quick Appliqué (page 33)	• Plain paper • Washable school glue or Roxanne's Glue-Baste-It • Scotch Restickable Glue Stick	• Any shape	• Machine zigzag, hem stitch, satin stitch, or hand stitch • May stitch edges before or after layering quilt sandwich	• May prewash fabrics to avoid bleeding. • May soak or wash after quilting to remove glue • Finished quilt OK to wash or dry-clean	1	1
Turned Edge Appliqué Using Spray Fusible (page 37)	• Freezer paper • Starch 606 Spray and Fix fusible adhesive	• Gentle shapes without deep curves	• Machine zigzag, hem stitch, satin stitch, or hand stitch • May stitch before or after layering quilt sandwich	• Prewash fabrics (optional) • After appliqué is stitched down, OK to wash or dry-clean	3–5 Edges of appliqué pieces are firmer than middle	3

Appliqué Method	Supplies Required*	Best For	Sewing Recommendations	Washing Recommendations	Softness (1 = soft to 5 = firm)	Difficulty (1 = easy to 5 = complex)
Turned Edge Reverse Appliqué (page 41)	• Freezer paper, interfacing, or hand-stitching supplies	• Gentle shapes	• Machine zigzag, hem stitch, satin stitch, or hand stitch • Stitch before layering quilt sandwich	• Prewash fabrics (optional) • Finished quilt OK to wash or dry-clean	• 1 without interfacing, or 4 with interfacing	3
Turned Edge Appliqué Using Interfacing (page 45)	• Interfacing	• Gentle shapes without deep curves	• Machine straight stitch then zigzag, hem stitch, straight stitch, satin stitch • Hand stitch	• Prewash fabrics (optional) • Finished quilt OK to wash or dry-clean	• 3–5 Depends on thickness of interfacing	3
Raw Edge Cut-and-Glue Appliqué (page 54)	• Washable school glue or Roxanne's Glue-Baste-It Bottle with small tip or toothpick	• Any shape	• Machine zigzag, straight stitch, blanket stitch, or satin stitch • Stitch after layering appliqué or after layering quilt sandwich	• Prewash fabrics (optional) • Washing not recommended; washing will fray raw edges	1	1
Raw Edge Appliqué Using Fusible Web (page 58)	• Fusible web (see Rating Chart page 83)	• Any shape	• Machine zigzag, straight stitch, blanket stitch, or satin stitch the edges • May stitch after layering quilt sandwich	• Prewash fabrics (optional) • Washing not recommended; washing will fray raw edges	• 2–5 Depends on thickness of fusible web	2
Raw Edge 3-Dimensional *Broderie Perse* Appliqué (page 61)	• Fusible web	• Any shape	• May machine zigzag, hem stitch, or satin stitch raw edges • Stitch appliqué onto quilt top after quilting	• Prewash fabrics (optional) • Washing not recommended; washing will fray raw edges	• 2–5 Depends on thickness of fusible web	• 1–2 Depends on edge treatment
Classic Needle-Turn Hand Appliqué (page 64)	• Hand-sewing needle (sharps, quilters, or milliners sizes 10 to 12), Thimble, Pins (thin and sharp)	• Gentle shapes • Deep curves, narrow stems, and sharp points after experience	• Hand stitch	• Prewash fabrics (optional) • Finished quilt OK to wash or dry-clean	1	2

*Most appliqué supplies can be purchased at your local quilt shop, fabric store, or office/school supply store.

Turned Edge Machine Appliqué

Mount Banner by Laurel Anderson, 38" × 32"

Turned edge appliqué mimics hand appliqué. In this technique, the edges of the appliqué shapes are turned to the wrong side of the piece, creating a crisp, folded seam along the piece's edge. The finished appliqué gives a classic look that is durable and washable. I use this method frequently because of these design qualities.

My quilt *Mount Banner* exemplifies the use of turned edge appliqué techniques. This technique requires a bit more work, but the results are especially helpful for projects that will see a lot of washing and/or wear, such as bed quilts, because the turned edges prevent fraying.

This section presents several ways to accomplish turned edge appliqué using a sewing machine. The wonderful thing about these methods is that they can produce sharp and narrow points. For each of the turned edge techniques provided in this book, a pattern template using plain paper,

freezer paper, or interfacing is used to stabilize the fabric shape. The fabric edges are turned over the template and held in place with starch, glue, or stitching. The primary difference between each technique is how the turned edges are held in place on the back side of the template. Use the starch method (page 24) for gentle curves and the gluestick method (page 29) for sharp curves or angles. Paper templates also allow you to create large, very complex designs.

Turned edge appliqué methods require the most steps, with the most difficult step being the machine stitching (blind, zigzag, or other side-to-side type stitching) on curved lines. As you work through these techniques, be willing to practice a couple of times with each. The more comfortable you are with the techniques, the better you will be able to judge which will work best for your needs.

Basics

The basic steps are to cut out each fabric shape, with a plain or freezer paper backing, and place it face up on the placement guide. Stand back and evaluate it for color or value mistakes. If you find any mistakes, just remove the freezer paper from the back of the offending fabric and iron it onto another fabric. It is much easier to change an offending fabric at this point than after it's been stitched. Sometimes I do this several times before I stitch the pieces together, because once sewn in place, mistakes must be "unsewn" with a seam ripper. This can be labor intensive. With the Turned Edge Quick Appliqué method (page 33), glue holds the shapes together, so sewing is not required until all the appliqué pieces are in place. Mistakes during the Quick Appliqué assembly can be easily fixed by moistening the pieces with water and pulling them apart, then adding a new piece in its place.

PREWASHING

Several of the techniques use starch or glue to assemble the appliqué. For these techniques, the assembled quilt top may be washed after assembly to remove the glue or starch residue. I recommend that for these techniques, all fabrics be prewashed or colorfastness. Prewash the fabrics and batting in warm to hot water. Use Synthrapol fabric detergent and a Shout Color Catcher sheet to capture the dye in the wash water. Prewashing minimizes irregular shrinkage and color bleeding.

TEMPLATES AND PLACEMENT GUIDES

When you're ready to start working on these projects, don't cut apart the original patterns. Instead, make a copy by tracing the design using a lightbox or window. If necessary, you can tape several sheets of plain paper together to make one large sheet to accommodate the entire design.

A reverse copy, or mirror image, of the templates is necessary for turned edge techniques using starch, gluestick, and spray fusible and for the reverse appliqué method. To make a reverse copy of the templates, first use a light table or window to trace a copy of the template to use as a placement guide. Next, turn the placement guide over, traced side down on the light table. With a clean sheet of paper, trace the placement guide in reverse to use as a template.

Remember to include the numbering when you trace the pattern pieces. The numbers indicate the sequential order in which the pieces are assembled. To simplify the quilt's assembly, make colored crosshatch marks on your pattern templates before cutting out the individual shapes. The numbered order of the templates and the crosshatch marks will aid in quickly aligning shapes during assembly.

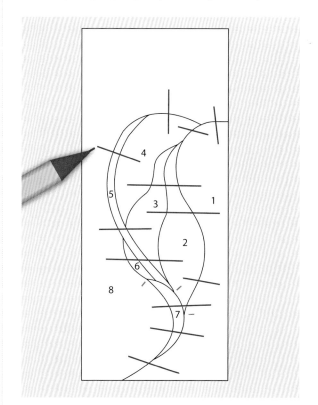

Crosshatch marks

TURNED EDGES

When assembling the appliqué shapes, only one side of each seam allowance is turned under. Along straight edges or very gentle curves, the turned under edge would be the piece on top or the edge of the adjoining piece with the next number in the order.

On more deeply curved appliqué lines, it is easier to turn under convex edges than concave edges. Think of a convex curve as being the hill and the concave curve as the valley. The appliqué fabric on convex (hill) curves will fold under easily onto the paper template behind it. Along concave (valley) curves, clip the seam allowance to make the turning under easier.

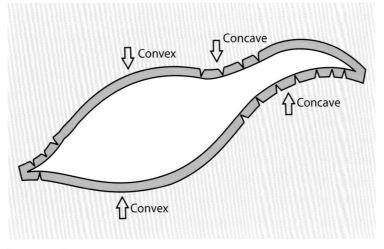

Concave and convex curves

In the order of appliquéing, some shapes have edges that are on top of one piece and under another. On these shapes, a clip in the seam allowance is taken to allow one part of the edge seam to turn under while the other part is left unturned. I have included tick marks in my templates to indicate the placement of these special turned edges. Remember to copy the tick marks when tracing paper copies.

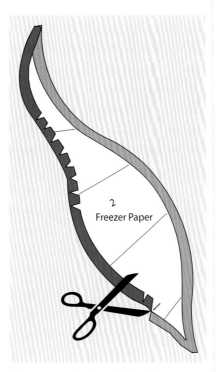

2
Freezer Paper

Clip curves and snip at tick mark.

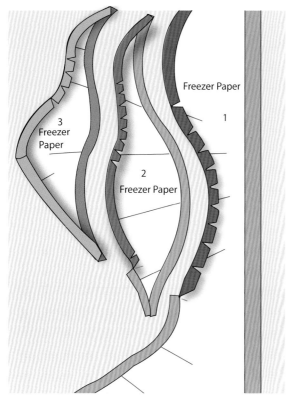

Appliqué shape with turned and unturned edges

The general rule is to add a ¼-inch seam allowance along all turned edges. Add a ½-inch seam allowance along the straight outer edges of the background appliqué. The ½-inch seam around the outer edges will be trimmed to straighten the quilt before adding the borders or finishing the quilt top.

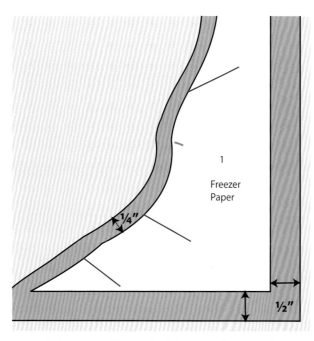

Leave ¼″ along curved lines and ½″ along straight outer edges.

THREAD

The most important thing to remember about thread is to match its color to the piece being appliquéd. This is especially true when stitches are invisible. When I stitch the pieces together, I use a high-quality polyester monofilament thread, also called invisible thread. Nylon monofilament thread melts when ironed and can ruin your work! Although polyester can also melt, it withstands much higher temperatures than nylon. Use smoke-colored monofilament for dark fabrics and clear for light-colored fabric. When one piece is dark and the other is pastel, match the thread color to the patch on the top, using smoke for dark and clear for pastel or medium-colored fabrics. When stitching with monofilament thread, use a neutral-colored thread for the bobbin.

Drafting Turned Edge Appliqué Designs

Years ago, I used to work with stained glass. Glass cuts best in straight lines. Because of the nature of glass, stained-glass patterns are drawn with lines leading away from all angles and tight curves. These lines are used as design elements to enhance the visual flow of the overall pattern. Machine appliqué with freezer paper lends itself to many of the best stained-glass design techniques. A wonderful floral bouquet pattern can be set within a swirling, curved background. The large amount of background detail stitches together quickly by machine. The background can be made up of many fabrics or just one. When I choose only one, I usually choose a tone-on-tone that will blur and hide the seams. For the *Whisper of Spring quilt* on page 76, I created a sky of half-circles. I like the way this gives mystery and movement to the design. It also cuts the sky into smaller pieces, so the patterns will fit on fat quarters of fabric.

I've always wanted the freedom to create my own designs, but I am not good at drawing. So I've learned to cheat! Instead of drawing my own flowers, I photograph them. I can trace the images and use them as patterns for quilting. *Inherit the Love* (page 76) is a quilt I made in a class by Lura Schwarz Smith. She had us trace our photo onto transparency plastic and use an overhead projector to project our image onto our full-sized pattern paper. I do the same with the computer program Adobe Illustrator.

After taking a class at the local junior college, I was able to trace my photographs in Illustrator, and then turn off the photograph layer and have a perfect pattern. In Illustrator, I can resize the pattern and place it in a different setting. The printer interface has an option for tiling. Tiling prints a large design onto several pages that can be taped together to equal a full-size pattern.

A low-tech way to do the same thing is to place graph paper over your image and trace the shape onto the graph paper. Choose the finished size of your design. On a full-sized sheet of paper, draw a grid with as many squares as your graph paper pattern. Number each row on both pages. Working square-by-square, redraw the pattern onto the full-sized paper. Smooth out the curves and go over the final drawing with a black marker.

If you're adapting a pattern for machine appliqué, draw lines through the background to continue the lines in the existing design elements. The tip of a curved iris leaf would extend as a curved line through the background. The iris leaf should be sewn to one side of the background and then the other. This order of assembly eliminates the need for turning under the fabric around the sharp leaf point. Think about this when you choose the order of assembly. Flowers with rounded curves can be assembled as separate units and sewn on top. Or, you may stitch them into the background. I have done them both ways.

Also, when adapting patterns for appliqué, add arrows to one side of each line to mark which seam allowance to turn under. Since the concave curves are harder to turn under and require clipping, whenever possible avoid turned edges on concave areas of shapes.

Whisper of Spring by Laurel Anderson, 72" × 18"

Turned Edge Appliqué Using Starch

The wonderful thing about this method is that it can make sharp and narrow points. It is possible to make large, very complex designs using this method. With this technique, freezer paper templates are ironed to the back of the appliqué fabric. The fabric pieces are cut larger than the templates, and then the raw edges are turned under, secured, and pressed with liquid starch (see Turned Edges, page 21). The starch may be washed out after assembly, so prewashing fabrics is recommended for colorfastness. Do not use this method for fabrics that bleed color.

The project for this technique is presented in two parts. In this chapter, I demonstrate how to construct the background of the tulip quilt. The sharp, narrow leaves are a perfect application for this freezer paper and starch method. Instructions to appliqué the tulip are presented in the following chapter, Turned Edge Appliqué Using Gluestick, on page 29.

I made this tulip quilt in many colors and variations. See Gallery, pages 72–82, for color inspirations.

Orange tulips inspired this project pattern.

Turned Edge Appliqué Using Starch

TULIP QUILT

FINISHED SIZE: 9″ × 22″

Golden Emperor Tulip by Laurel Anderson

Supplies

Choose fabrics that provide contrast between background and flowers. Prewash and press all fabrics. Hand-dyed and batik fabrics can provide deep, rich color variations (see Hand Dyeing Your Own Fabric, page 89).

- 10″ × 10″ square fabric for tulip petals
- 10″ × 10″ square each of 3 different fabrics for stem and leaves
- 1 fat quarter for background
- ⅜ yard fabric for outer border
- ⅛ yard fabric for border detail strip (optional; see page 28)
- ¼ yard fabric for binding
- ⅓ yard fabric for backing
- Batting, 11″ × 24″
- Plain paper, 11″ × 17″ or larger, for the placement guide
- Freezer paper for templates
- Scissors for paper and for fabric
- Iron and pad
- Fabric starch and small container (The cover of a spray can or a small artist's paint palette works well.)
- Paintbrush or cotton swabs
- Scotch tape
- Polyester monofilament (invisible) for top thread in smoke and clear colors
- Neutral-colored thread for bobbin
- Tweezers
- Rotary cutter, ruler, and mat
- Synthrapol fabric detergent
- Shout Color Catcher sheet

Preparing the Pattern Pieces

1. Use a pencil and lightbox or window to trace 1 copy of the Tulip Quilt background template (pullout P1) on plain paper to use as a placement guide. Using the same method, turn the placement guide traced side down and trace 1 copy in reverse on the dull side of freezer paper. Include numbers and tick marks on both copies. Note that each piece is numbered and will be appliquéd in order.

2. On the freezer paper pattern, with a colored pen, make 1″-long crosshatch marks, perpendicular to all adjoining piece lines. These colored marks will help as you reassemble the pieces once they are ironed to fabric (see Templates and Placement Guides, page 20).

Putting It Together

1. Cut out pattern pieces 1 and 2 on the lines from the freezer paper pattern. Iron the shiny side of the freezer paper to the *wrong* side of the fabric for 3 seconds on the dry cotton setting. Leave at least ¾″ between each pattern piece. Place the stems along the bias grain of the fabric. Place the square outer edges of the pattern piece along the straight fabric grain.

2. Cut out each fabric piece, remembering to add ¼″ seam allowance along all curved edges and ½″ seam allowance along the straight outer edges. The ½″ seam around the outer edges will be trimmed to straighten the quilt before adding the borders (see Turned Edges, on page 21).

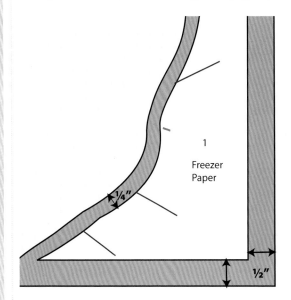

1
Freezer Paper

¼″

½″

Leave ¼″ along curved lines and ½″ along straight lines.

3. Choose one side of each adjoining seam to turn under. The other side will slide under the folded side, and the folded edge will be stitched down. The easiest side to turn under is the side with the most convex shape. Concave shapes must have their seam allowance clipped enough so they will lie flat when turned under (see Turned Edges, page 21). Clip seam allowances at each tick mark and along concave curves. The tick marks indicate where the seam allowance changes from flat to turned under.

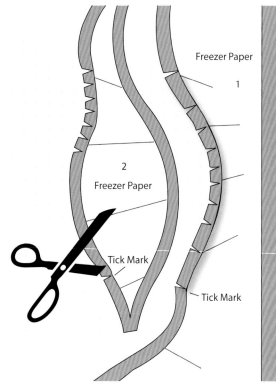

Clip seam allowances.

4. Spray starch into a small container. Using the cotton swab or paintbrush, apply starch to the seam allowances that will be turned under.

5. Turn under the starched edges, covering the freezer paper behind them. Iron with a cotton setting for about 3 seconds to secure the edges in place.

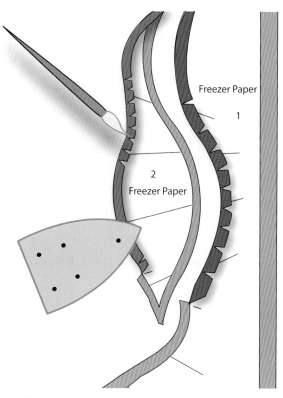

Apply starch and turn under edges.

6. Use the colored crosshatch marks and placement guide to position and align pieces 1 and 2.

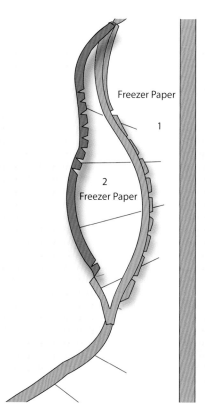

Align adjoining pieces, using the pattern as a guide.

7. Pins will distort the freezer paper, so align the pieces and tape them together. Place tape on the freezer paper side near the edge of the seam allowance away from the stitching line. Or place the tape on the front of the fabric and remove it just before stitching over it.

Scotch tape: another common appliqué tool.

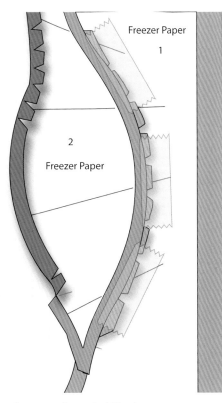

Tape the pieces together to hold in place.

8. With monofilament thread in the needle and neutral-colored thread in the bobbin (see Thread, page 22), zigzag or hem stitch over the seamline. Use smoke-colored thread when sewing dark fabric to a dark fabric. When one piece is dark and the other is pastel, match the thread color to the patch on the top. Use smoke for dark and clear for pastel or medium-colored fabrics. Instead of monofilament, colored thread may be matched to the background piece.

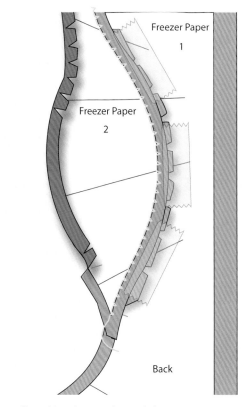

Stitch seam line with a zigzag or hem stitch.

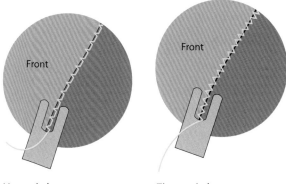

Hem stitch   Zigzag stitch

9. Remove the tape but leave the freezer paper.

10. Cut out the next piece. Prepare and sew it in place using Steps 1–9 until the background is completed.

11. Remove the freezer paper from the completed appliqué background.

12. Appliqué the tulip flower to the background. See Turned Edge Appliqué Using Gluestick, page 29, for instructions.

Finishing the Quilt

1. Soak the appliquéd quilt top in cool water to dissolve the starch and glue. Place a teaspoon of Synthrapol and a Shout Color Catcher sheet in the container to reduce the chance of color bleed. Rinse gently. Remove any remaining freezer paper. Use tweezers to remove the points of paper that break off. Iron until flat and dry. Trim any seam allowances that show a shadow through pale fabric.

2. Use a rotary cutter and ruler to trim and square the quilt top to 6½″ × 14½″. Add optional border detail strips, if desired (see box below).

3. Use the border fabric to cut 2 rectangles 6½″ × 4½″ for the top and bottom borders and 2 rectangles 2″ × 22½″ for the side borders.

4. Sew the top and bottom borders to the tulip panel using a ¼″ seam allowance. Then sew each side border to the quilt top.

5. Quilt the finished top as desired.

6. Add binding, sleeve, and label.

❀ OPTIONAL BORDER DETAIL STRIPS

An optional detail strip may be placed between the tulip panel and the border or between the border and the binding.

Cut two detail strips 1 inch × width of fabric. Fold each in half, lengthwise, wrong sides together. Press. Align and pin the raw edges of one detail strip with the top edge of the quilt panel, trimming excess. Use a scant ¼-inch seam allowance to sew the strip to the top of the quilt. Use the second strip in the same manner, and sew the bottom detail strip to the quilt. Use the leftover strips to add the side details.

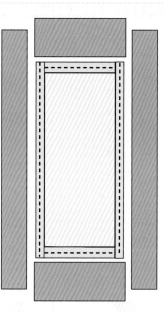

Sew detail strips before adding borders.

Turned Edge Appliqué Using Gluestick

The gluestick method is similar to the starch method (page 24), but the water-soluble (washable) gluestick provides more control in turning the fabric under tight curves and sharp points. When turning the appliqué edges, the washable gluestick holds the fabric edges over the freezer paper.

The project for this technique is presented in two parts. In this chapter, I demonstrate how to make the tulip flower. The gluestick method is best used in patterns with deep curves. This works well for flowers and small pieces. Look for a gluestick labeled *acid-free* and *washable*. Prewash the fabrics because the glue may be washed out after assembly, allowing the freezer paper to be removed. Prewashing reduces color bleed and uneven shrinking.

Instructions for the background panel are presented in the previous chapter, Turned Edge Appliqué Using Starch (page 24). For some projects, like the tulip quilts, you may find yourself using both of these techniques to achieve the desired results. Practice both the starch and the glue and you'll have a well-stocked toolbox for your projects.

PRACTICE:
Turned Edge Appliqué Using Gluestick

TULIP QUILT

FINISHED SIZE: 9″ × 22″

Blushing Lady Tulip by Laurel Anderson

Supplies

- Fabrics (see Turned Edge Appliqué Using Starch, page 24)
- Freezer paper
- Washable gluestick (any that is acid-free and washes out)
- Toothpick or other stylus
- Polyester monofilament (invisible) for top thread in smoke and clear colors
- Neutral-colored thread for bobbin
- Scissors for paper and for fabric
- Scotch tape

Preparing the Pattern Pieces

1. Use a pencil and lightbox or window to trace 1 copy of the Tulip template (pullout P1) to use as a placement guide. Using the same method, turn the placement guide traced side down and trace 1 copy in reverse on the dull side of freezer paper. Include numbers and tick marks on both copies. Note that each piece is numbered and will be appliquéd in order.

2. On the freezer paper pattern, with a colored pen, make 1"-long crosshatch marks, perpendicular to all adjoining piece lines. These colored marks will help when reassembling the pieces once they are ironed to fabric (see Templates and Placement Guides, page 20).

Putting It Together

1. Assemble the appliqué background panel, following the steps in Turned Edge Appliqué Using Starch on page 24.

2. Cut out Tulip pattern pieces 1 and 2 on the lines from the freezer paper pattern. Iron the shiny side of the freezer paper to the *wrong* side of the fabric for 3 seconds on the dry cotton setting. Leave at least ¾" between each pattern piece.

3. Cut out each fabric piece, remembering to add ¼" seam allowance along all edges.

4. Clip seam allowances at each tick mark and along concave curves (see Turned Edges, page 21). The tick marks indicate where the seam allowance changes from flat to turned under.

5. One side of each seam must be turned under. The curves that do not have to be clipped are the best choice (see Turned Edges, page 21). Apply gluestick to the seam allowances that will be turned under. Then fold the fabric edges over the freezer paper. Use a toothpick or other small tool to help smooth out the curves.

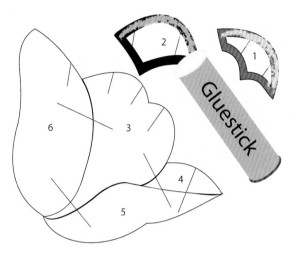

Gluestick holds the folded fabric edges in place.

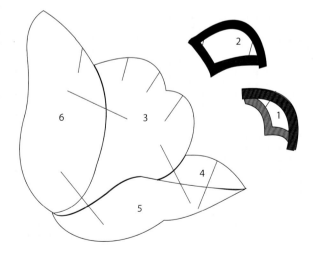

Fold the seam over the freezer paper.

6. Repeat steps 2–5 for the next adjacent piece.

7. Apply gluestick along the seam allowance to the second (adjacent) overlapping piece.

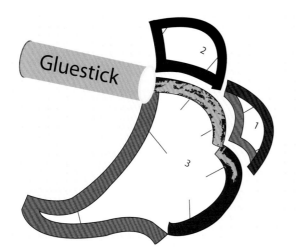

Use gluestick to join appliqué pieces together.

8. Use the pattern placement guide and freezer paper template crosshatch marks to align adjacent pieces.

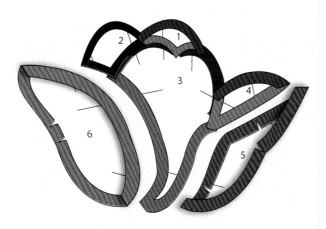

Use crosshatch marks to align pieces.

9. Add the remaining pieces in numerical order in the same manner.

10. Allow the glue to dry. Use polyester monofilament thread in the needle and neutral thread in the bobbin (see Thread, page 22). Zigzag or hem stitch along the fold line of each overlapped set of pieces. Use smoke-colored thread when sewing a dark fabric to a dark fabric. When one piece is dark and the other is pastel, match the thread color to the patch on the top, smoke for dark and clear for pastel or medium-colored fabrics.

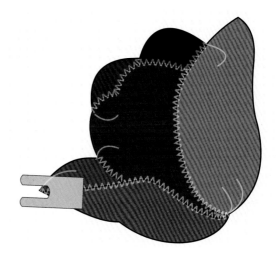

Use a hem stitch or a zigzag stich to sew the pieces together.

11. Place the assembled unit of appliqué on the background panel. Tape the appliqué unit in place and zigzag or hem stitch around the unit's outer edges. Pull the thread ends to the back.

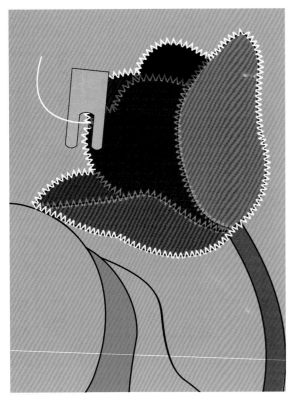

Zigzag stitch around perimeter of appliqué unit.

12. Cut away the background behind the appliqué unit, allowing a ¼" seam allowance.

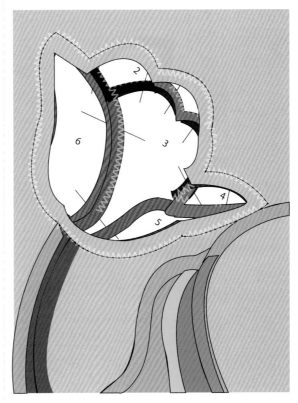

Trim background only to remove freezer paper template.

13. See Finishing the Quilt, on page 28, for directions on completing the Tulip Quilt.

Turned Edge Quick Appliqué

This turned-edge technique is for the very busy artist. It combines the durability of turned edge appliqué with two types of glue for speed. A whole quilt top can be assembled without a sewing machine. The final quilting is all the stitching needed.

Although similar to the starch (page 24) and gluestick (page 29) techniques, this method uses plain paper and Scotch Restickable Glue Stick instead of freezer paper. The Scotch Restickable Glue Stick is similar to the adhesive on the back of sticky notes and holds the paper in place on the front of the appliqué fabric. (*Note:* I have not had the same success using Elmer's brand of restickable glue or the Spray and Fix 404 or 505.) Small dots of liquid school glue are used instead of stitching to hold the pieces together. Any mistakes during the appliqué assembly can be quickly fixed by moistening the pieces with water and pulling them apart. The glue can be rinsed out after quilting, so pre-washing fabrics is recommended for colorfastness. Do not use this method for fabrics that bleed color.

The project for this technique is presented in two parts. In this chapter, I demonstrate the use of Turned Edge Quick Appliqué for the leaves and background of the Iris Panel Quilt. Instructions for appliqué of the iris flower are presented in the project for Raw Edge Cut-and-Glue Appliqué on page 54.

PRACTICE:
Turned Edge Quick Appliqué
Iris Panel Quilt

FINISHED SIZE: 9˝ × 21˝

Pink Iris by Laurel Anderson

Supplies

Choose fabrics that provide contrast between background and flowers. Prewash and press all fabrics. Hand-dyed and batik fabrics can provide deep, rich color variations (see Hand Dyeing Your Own Fabric, page 89).

- ⅛ yard fabric, or a variety of 5″ squares, for iris petals
- Small scrap orange, yellow, or white fabric for iris center
- 1 fat quarter for leaves
- 1 fat quarter for background
- ⅓ yard fabric for border
- ¼ yard fabric for binding
- ⅓ yard fabric for backing
- Batting, 11″ × 24″
- Plain copy paper, 11″ × 17″ or larger, for templates and placement guide
- Scissors for paper and for fabric
- Scotch Restickable Glue Stick
- School glue (white or clear), Roxanne Glue-Baste-It, or washable gluestick
- Plastic wrap
- Towels
- Iron and pad
- Synthrapol fabric detergent
- Shout Color Catcher sheet

Preparing the Pattern Pieces

1. Use a pencil and a lightbox or window to trace 2 copies of the Iris Panel Quilt background template (pullout P1) on plain paper. One copy will be used as a placement guide and the other for the appliqué templates. Include numbers on both copies. Note that each piece is numbered and will be appliquéd in order.

2. Spread restickable glue on the back (unmarked) side of the uncut traced appliqué templates. Do *not* apply glue to the placement guide. Allow the glue to dry for about a minute.

Putting It Together

1. Cut out each template piece. Place each template on the ***front*** side of the appropriate fabric, sticky side down. (The restickable glue should adhere and pull off without leaving adhesive on the fabric.) Leave at least ¾″ between each pattern piece.

2. Cut out each fabric piece, remembering to add ¼″ seam allowance along all curved edges and ½″ seam allowance along the straight outer edges. (The ½″ seam around the outer edges will be trimmed to straighten the quilt before adding the borders; see Turned Edges, page 21.) Leave the pattern piece stuck to the fabric.

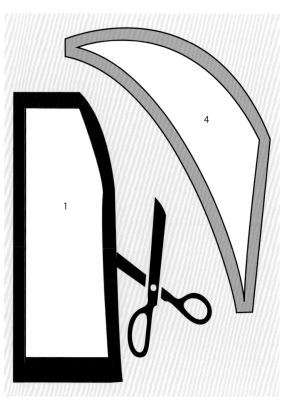

Add a ¼″ seam allowance to the pattern pieces.

3. One side of each seam must be turned under. The curves that do not have to be clipped are the best choice (see Turned Edges, page 21). With the pattern piece stuck to the right side of the fabric, turn the seam allowance under, toward the wrong side. Match the fold of the fabric with the edge of the paper pattern and glue it in place with small dots of glue. Use enough adhesive to create a smooth edge. The glue may be rinsed out after quilting.

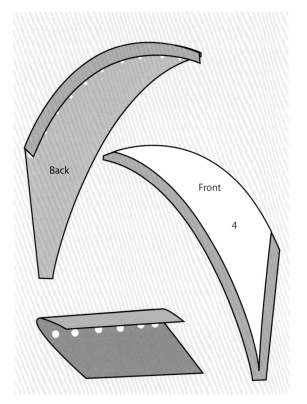

Glue edges to wrong side of appliqué fabric piece.

4. Use the placement guide to lay the pieces in the correct position.

> 🌼 Put a layer of plastic wrap over the placement guide to prevent it from getting damaged.

5. Apply small dots of glue to the unturned edge of the adjoining seam allowance. Align the adjoining pieces, allowing the glue to hold the pieces in place. Tuck the raw edges of the leaf points behind the adjoining shape, and glue.

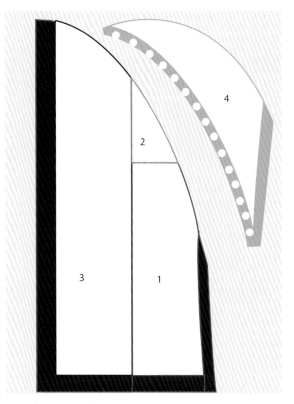

Glue the unturned seam allowances.

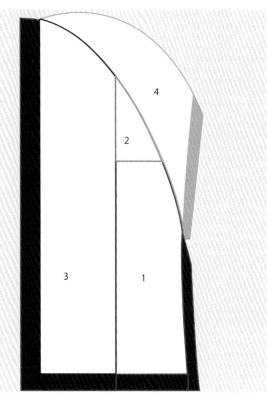

Join the pieces together.

6. Continue adding pieces in numerical order using Steps 2–5 until the whole background is assembled with glue. Evaluate the color and fabric choices from the back. If you don't like your fabric choices, moisten the seams with water, wait a minute, and gently peel apart the pieces. Restick the template piece to new fabric and glue in place as before.

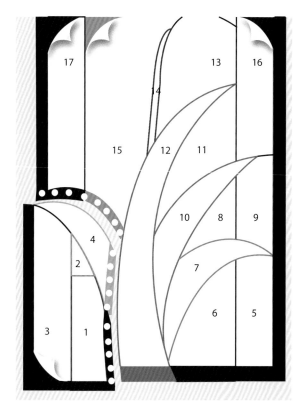

Glue the next seam.

7. Remove the sticky-backed paper template pieces. If any paper remains on the fabric, moisten it with water. Wait a minute and then gently scrape it away.

8. Appliqué the iris flower to the background. See Raw Edge Cut-and-Glue Appliqué, page 54, for instructions.

Finishing the Quilt

1. Trim and square the appliquéd quilt top to 9½″ × 22½″.

2. Layer the quilt with prewashed batting and backing.

3. Quilt the finished top as desired. Keep in mind that the final quilting may be the only stitching holding the appliqué pieces in place. Make sure quilting stitches catch all edges and seams of the appliqué to secure them in place.

4. Optional: Soak the finished quilt in warm water with a teaspoon of Synthrapol detergent and a Shout Color Catcher sheet. Rinse the quilt in clean water. Roll the quilt in towels and squeeze out excess water. Lay the quilt flat on dry towels. Spread it out, as necessary, until it has straight edges and right-angled corners. Pin in place. Allow to dry completely. Press from the back if needed. The glue may also be left in the finished quilt, if removal isn't preferred.

5. Add binding, sleeve, and label.

Turned Edge Appliqué Using Spray Fusible

This technique is very similar to the Turned Edge Appliqué Using Starch (page 24), with a combination of freezer paper, starch, and spray fusible adhesive. The main difference is that instead of sewing the appliqué to the background, a fusible spray adhesive is applied to the back of the pieces along the seam allowance and then fused in place. The fused shape will not have enough adhesive to survive washing, but with care, it will survive until quilting. The edges may be stitched before or during final quilting.

In this project, a fusible spray method will be used to appliqué the dogwood flowers to the background fabric. Any shape that can be starched around freezer paper may be used in this technique. Instructions for adding the Faux Facing Technique for Borders are included on page 88.

Check the Appendix for a comparison chart on fusible products (page 83). Remember to carefully read all spray adhesive instructions and use in a well-ventilated area. You are not allowed to glue your lungs with Spray and Fix. Quilters are valuable. We can't spare any, and especially not you!

PRACTICE:
Turned Edge Appliqué Using Spray Fusible
DOGWOOD QUILT

FINISHED SIZE: 16″ × 11″

Dogwood **by Laurel Anderson**

Supplies

Choose fabrics that provide contrast between background and flowers. Prewash and press all fabrics. Hand-dyed fabrics can provide deep, rich color variations; consider using them instead of commercial fabrics (see Hand Dyeing Your Own Fabric, page 89).

- 1 fat quarter for petals
- 5" × 5" square fabric for flower centers
- 5" × 5" square fabric for stems
- 3" × 3" square fabric for leaf
- 13" × 18" fabric for background
- 13" × 18" fabric for border
- 13" × 18" lightweight (nonstretchy) fusible interfacing for border
- ½ yard fabric for backing
- Batting, 14" × 19"
- Freezer paper for templates
- Plain copy paper, 11" × 17" or larger, for placement guide
- Fabric starch and small container (The cover of a spray can or a small artist's paint palette works well.)
- Paintbrush or cotton swabs
- 606 Spray and Fix fusible adhesive
- Scissors for paper and for fabric
- Newspaper or paper towel
- Iron and pad
- 2 appliqué transparent pressing sheets, silicone sheets, or parchment paper
- Scotch tape (optional)
- Matching thread for needle and bobbin
- Beads for flower centers (optional)

Preparing the Pattern Pieces

1. Use a pencil and a lightbox or window to trace 1 copy of the Dogwood Quilt template (pullout P1) on plain paper to use as a placement guide. Using the same method, turn the placement guide traced side down and trace 1 copy in reverse on the dull side of freezer paper. Include numbers and tick marks on both copies. Note that each piece is numbered and will be appliquéd in order.

Putting It Together

1. Cut out the pattern pieces on the lines from the freezer paper pattern. Iron the shiny side to the **wrong** side of the fabric for 3 seconds on the dry cotton setting. Leave ¾" fabric between freezer paper pieces. Cut out each fabric shape, adding ¼" seam allowance along all edges.

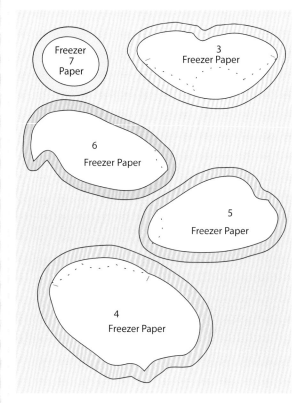

Add a ¼" seam allowance.

2. Clip seam allowances at each tick mark and along concave overlapping curves (see Turned Edges, page 21). The tick marks are where the seam allowance changes from flat to turned under.

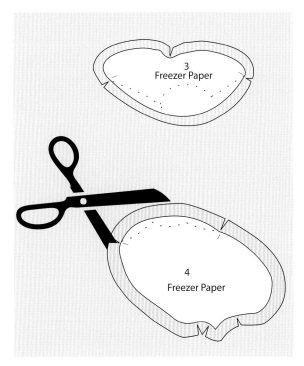

Clip the seam allowance at tick marks.

3. Spray starch into a small container. Using the cotton swab or paintbrush, apply starch to the seam allowances that will be turned under.

4. One side of each seam must be turned under. The curves that do not have to be clipped are the best choice (see Turned Edges, page 21). Turn under the starched seam allowances covering the freezer paper behind them. Iron with a cotton setting for 3–4 seconds to secure the seams in place.

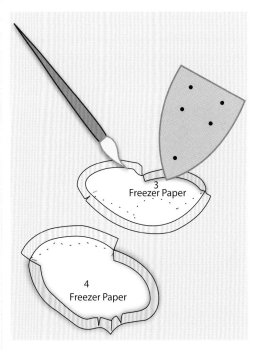

Apply starch to the seam allowance.

5. In a well-ventilated location, cover the work surface with newspapers or paper towels. Place the prepared fabric shapes, freezer paper facing up, on the covered work surface. Following the manufacturer's directions, apply 606 Spray and Fix to the back of the pieces, coating the turned seam allowances. Allow shapes to dry. Shake off any loose adhesive powder.

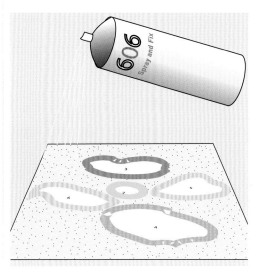

Apply fusible spray to the seam allowances.

6. Lay the placement guide on the ironing pad, writing side up. Cover the placement guide with a transparent pressing sheet or parchment paper. Arrange the sprayed appliqué pieces face up on the guide. Carefully align the pieces with the placement guide, making sure the turned under edges are placed on top of the unfolded seam allowances.

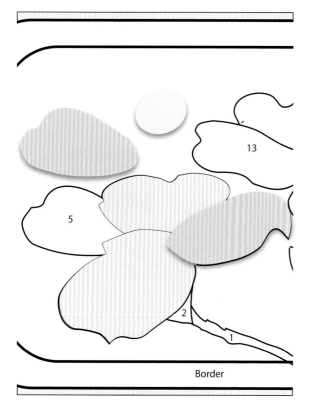

Position appliqué pieces on placement guide.

7. Place another pressing sheet or parchment paper over the arranged pieces, being careful not to disturb the alignment. With the iron on cotton setting, press for 30 seconds. Allow to cool. Remove the pressing sheet. Remove the freezer paper templates. If the freezer paper is difficult to grab, stick one end of a piece of tape to it and pull up.

8. Place the fused appliqué unit in position on the background fabric. Cover with a pressing sheet and press for 30–45 seconds. Allow to cool. Check for a strong bond. Stitch the edges of the appliqué to secure in place or wait for the final quilting.

Finishing the Quilt

Add a curved border and finish the quilt using Faux Facing Technique for Borders on page 88.

> ❀ OPTIONAL EMBELLISHMENT: Before adding the backing, sew beads to dogwood flower centers.

Turned Edge Reverse Appliqué

In traditional appliqué, a shaped piece is stitched on top of a background. With reverse appliqué, a shape is cut away from the background layer, and the edges of the opening are stitched under, revealing the appliqué fabric underneath. Reverse appliqué is a very useful way to hide dark seam allowances so they don't darken a pale fabric. I also use reverse appliqué to create a smoother edge when the appliqué has many seams that are difficult to turn under and the background layer is not pieced. Reverse appliqué can also be used to sew a curved frame around a heavily seamed center.

This project adds a circle reverse-appliquéd sun to a finished background. The background appliqué is assembled using the Turned Edge Appliqué Using Starch (page 24) method. The iris flower and bud are then added using the Raw Edge Cut-and-Glue Appliqué (page 54) method. Once the background appliqué is finished, the background is then cut with turned edges revealing the sun appliqué beneath. The glue is washed out after assembly, so prewashing fabrics is recommended for colorfastness. Do not use this method for fabrics that bleed color.

PRACTICE:
Turned Edge Reverse Appliqué

RAIN QUILT

FINISHED SIZE: 29″ × 29″

Rain by Laurel Anderson

Supplies

Choose fabrics that provide contrast between background and flowers. Prewash and press all fabrics. Hand-dyed and batik fabrics can provide deep, rich color variations (see Hand Dyeing Your Own Fabric, page 89).

- 6″ × 6″ square each of 7–8 different fabrics for flower and bud
- 6″ × 18″ each of 6–7 different fabrics for stems and leaves
- 3″ × 3″ square fabric for sun
- 1 fat quarter each of 6 different fabrics for background
- 6″ × 20″ fabric for water
- 6″ × 10″ each of 5 fabrics for foreground
- ½ yard fabric for background border
- 1 yard fabric for cameo border facing, cut to 30″ × 30″
- ¼ yard fabric for detail strips
- 1 yard fabric for backing
- Batting, 31″ × 31″
- Freezer paper for templates
- Tracing paper or newsprint for facing template
- Plain copy paper, 11″ × 17″ or larger, for placement guide
- Starch and school glue, gluestick, or Roxanne Glue-Baste-It for turned edges
- Paintbrush or cotton swabs
- Scissors for paper and fabric
- Iron and pad
- Matching thread for needle and bobbin
- Shout Color Catcher sheet
- Tweezers
- Assorted beads of various shapes in clear, white, violet, lavender, and blue (optional)

Preparing the Pattern Pieces

1. Following the directions for Turned Edge Appliqué Using Starch, Preparing the Pattern Pieces, on page 25, prepare the placement guide and freezer paper templates for the Rain Quilt background template (pullout P4).

2. Following the directions for Raw Edge Cut-and-Glue Appliqué, Preparing the Pattern Pieces, on page 55, prepare the freezer paper templates for the Rain Quilt Flower and Bud templates (pullout P4).

3. Use a pencil and a lightbox or window to trace 1 copy of the Sun template (pullout P4), centered, on the dull side of a 5″ × 5″ piece of freezer paper. Fold the freezer paper on the drawn line and snip with sharp paper scissors. Insert the scissors in the slit and cut out the template shape following the line. (For an alternate method to appliqué perfect circles, see Turned Edge Appliqué Using Interfacing on page 45.)

4. Prepare the circle facing template by folding a 30″ × 30″ square of tracing paper or newsprint in half twice. Open the paper and use the fold lines to center and trace the 25½″ circle from the Rain Quilt background template. Cut the circle from the middle of the paper. Round the square corners to more easily attach the detail strip.

> The facing of the *Rain* quilt, shown on page 41, was created with square corners. For ease of assembly, facing templates and finishing directions for this project have rounded corners.

5. Trace 1 more copy of the Sun template on the dull side of freezer paper for the Sun pattern piece.

Putting It Together

1. Use the Rain Quilt background templates to appliqué the background, following the directions for Turned Edge Appliqué Using Starch, Putting It Together, on page 25. Remember to cut each fabric piece allowing ¼″ seam allowance along all curved edges and ½″ seam allowance along the straight outer edges. (The ½″ seam around the outer edges will be trimmed to straighten the quilt before adding the borders; see Turned Edges, on page 21.)

2. Appliqué the iris flower to the background, following the directions for Raw Edge Cut-and-Glue Appliqué on page 54.

3. Remove the freezer paper from behind the area that will get the sun appliqué.

Appliqué the Sun with Reverse Appliqué

The sun appliqué may be added using the Turned Edge Reverse Appliqué technique or the Turned Edge Appliqué Using Interfacing technique (page 45).

1. Position the square freezer paper Sun template, shiny side down, on the back of the appliqué background. Iron for 3 seconds on the dry cotton setting to secure in place.

2. Cut out the center opening of the fabric, allowing a ¼" seam allowance around the inside of the circle and being careful not to cut the freezer paper. Clip the seam allowances.

3. Use starch or glue to turn under the edges of the shape around the freezer paper. The edges will be turned to the *wrong* side of the background.

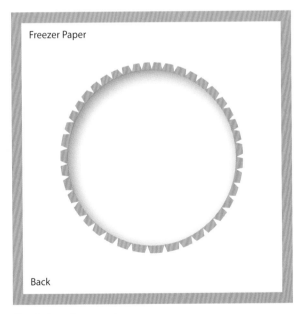

Clip circle and turn under seam.

4. Iron the circle freezer paper Sun pattern on the *wrong* side of the sun fabric. Cut out the fabric, allowing a ¼" seam allowance around all outside edges. Do not turn under the seams.

5. Apply small dots of glue to the turned edge of the background opening. Align the sun appliqué piece over the opening, allowing the glue to hold the pieces in place.

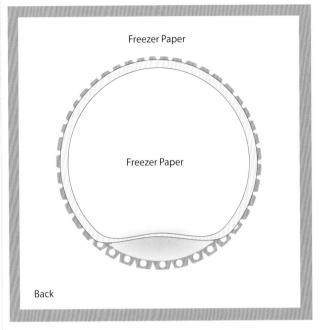

Position appliqué behind opening in background.

6. Stitch the appliqué in place along the fold line on the front of the appliquéd quilt top, or stitch in place when quilting, being careful to catch all seams.

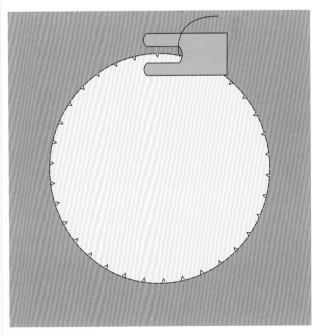

Stitch appliqué piece to background fabric.

✿ *Reverse appliqué a pale shape onto a dark background:*

When selecting fabrics, hold the pale fabric over the dark fabric to see if the dark fabric shows through the pale fabric. When choosing white fabrics, I use white sateen because it is thicker and less likely to show the color beneath. The sheen of the sateen also makes the white appear brighter.

Reverse appliqué heavy seams:

Heavy seams are hard to turn under smoothly. Turn under the background fabric instead and stitch it down.

Finishing the Quilt

1. Soak the appliquéd quilt top in cool water to dissolve the starch and glue. Place a Shout Color Catcher sheet in the container to reduce the chance of color bleed. Rinse gently. Remove the freezer paper. Use tweezers to remove the points of paper that break off. Iron until flat and dry. Trim any remaining seam allowances that show a shadow through pale fabric.

2. Trim the appliquéd top to 18½″ × 18½″.

3. Use the border fabric to cut 2 rectangles 6″ × 18½″ for the side borders and 2 rectangles 6″ × 29½″ for the top and bottom borders.

4. Sew the side borders to the appliquéd background using a ¼″ seam allowance. Then sew the top and bottom borders.

✿ OPTIONAL EMBELLISHMENT: Sew beads to flowers, to leaves, and in slanted rows for an impression of rain.

5. Finish the quilt with a circle opening facing, following Completing a Quilt with a Facing on page 84.

6. Quilt the finished top as desired.

Turned Edge Appliqué Using Interfacing

This turned edge technique using interfacing is perfect for making large shapes, such as perfect circles, and can simplify S-shaped curves. Use fusible interfacing, nonfusible interfacing, or wash-away stabilizer. All of the edges are turned under, with the interfacing providing added bulk around the seams. Stitch around the edges of each piece if the quilt will ever be washed. Fusible interfacing may adhere well enough that no additional stitching is needed until the quilting stage. The advantage of this method over any of the freezer paper methods is that there is no glue or starch to wash out.

Just about any large shape can be appliquéd with this technique. The project shows this method as an alternative to reverse appliqué of the sun in the *Rain* quilt (see Turned Edge Reverse Appliqué, page 41)

PRACTICE:
Turned Edge Appliqué Using Interfacing
RAIN QUILT

FINISHED SIZE: 29″ × 29″

Rain; sun detail by Laurel Anderson (full quilt on page 41)

Supplies

- Fabrics and Supplies (see Turned Edge Reverse Appliqué, page 41)

- Fusible or nonfusible interfacing

- Wash-away stabilizer (may be substituted for interfacing)

Preparing the Pattern Pieces

See Turned Edge Reverse Appliqué, page 41, for preparing the background and flower appliqué. The sun appliqué may be added using the Turned Edge Reverse Appliqué technique (page 41) or as follows using the Turned Edge Appliqué Using Interfacing.

1. Trace the Sun template pattern (pullout P4) onto the nonadhesive side of the interfacing.

2. Cut out the interfacing shape, allowing a ½" seam allowance.

Putting It Together

1. Pin the interfacing to the right side of the sun appliqué fabric. If using fusible interfacing, place the adhesive side facing the right side of the fabric. Do *not* fuse.

2. Sew along the drawn lines with a small stitch length, about 1.5.

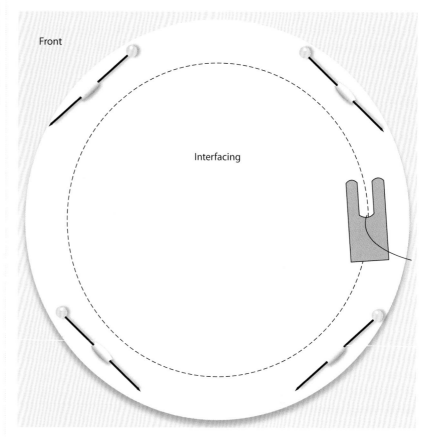

Sew interfacing to the right side of the appliqué fabric.

3. Cut out the fabric, allowing a ¼" seam allowance and clipping curves (trimming corners if necessary). Trim the interfacing, allowing a ⅛" seam allowance.

4. Pull the interfacing away from the fabric, and cut a slit near the middle of the interfacing, being careful not to cut the fabric.

Cut slit in the center of the interfacing.

5. Trim the interfacing to remove the middle, allowing a ½" seam allowance around the edges.

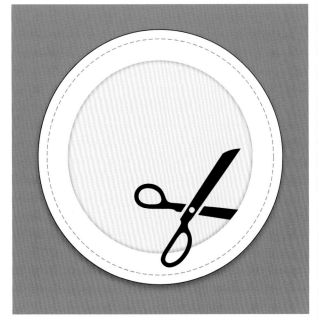

Remove the interfacing in the middle of the appliqué.

6. Turn the interfacing to the back side of the appliqué fabric, smoothing all curves and finger-pressing the edges flat.

7. Place the piece, interfacing down, onto the quilt background. Pin in place. Or, if using the fusible interfacing, fuse to the background fabric following the manufacturer's directions.

Press to fuse the appliqué in place.

8. Stitch around the edges of the appliqué piece using a machine stitch. If you prefer, you can skip this step and stitch the piece in place during the quilting process.

Finishing the Quilt

See Turned Edge Reverse Appliqué, Finishing the Quilt, on page 44.

Raw Edge Machine Appliqué

When an appliqué piece does not have a turned edge that creates a finished seam, it is called raw edged. There are many variations on creating raw edge appliqué, including fusible appliqué with stitched edges, *Broderie Perse*, and the easy Cut-and-Glue technique. Raw edge appliqué is fun and easy, and it's been gaining in popularity with designers who make incredibly intricate fabric paintings using raw edge techniques. The advantages of raw edge appliqué are how fast it can be accomplished (often, you just cut out the shape and adhere it to a background) and the design freedom it allows the quilter. Since you're not worrying about turning under a tiny, complex edge, you can get as intricate in cutting the fabric shapes as you can with a piece of paper. Because of this, a flower can be assembled and auditioned in many locations on the quilt before it is attached.

But, there are drawbacks to raw edge appliqué. The biggest is that over time the edges can fray and split. If you're working with a project that will be washed repeatedly, raw edge appliqué will start looking very fuzzy, even if it's stitched down. Of course, this texture can be considered part of the design of the project, so you'll have to judge for yourself if this will work for you. But, for those projects that will receive little or no washing and handling, like art quilts, wall quilts, or similar projects, raw edge appliqué can be just what the quilter ordered.

Basics

For raw edge appliqué, the basic steps are simple. Shapes are cut from the appliqué fabric and arranged on the background. Shapes are cut with a small seam allowance along the edges of adjoining pieces, allowing a small amount of overlap. In the Cut-and-Glue method (page 54), shapes are attached to the background with washable glue. The glue may be washed out when the quilt is complete. In the Fusible Web technique (page 58), fusible webbing is ironed to the back of the appliqué fabrics before the shapes are cut. The webbing-backed appliqué shapes are then fused to the background for permanent placement. In three-dimensional *Broderie Perse* (page 61), two layers of fabric are sandwiched with fusible web to make a double-sided fabric. This is cut into leaves and petals. Sew each shape down the middle to attach it to the finished quilt. Refer to the Fusible Product Comparison Chart on page 83 for more information about application of fusible products in appliqué.

PREWASHING

For the Cut-and-Glue method, the finished quilt can be washed to remove the glue. I recommend prewashing all fabrics for this technique to ensure colorfastness. Use Synthrapol detergent and a Shout Color Catcher sheet to capture the dye in the wash water.

TEMPLATES AND PLACEMENT GUIDES

Many raw edge techniques require the templates to be placed on the wrong side of the fabric and then cut from the fabric. In those methods, the templates need to be made in reverse, or mirror image, of the finished quilt design. In contrast, the techniques illustrated in this book position the templates on the right side of the fabric using restickable glue, thus eliminating the need to reverse the design when creating templates.

Most fusible web products have a paper backing (see Fusible Product Comparison Chart, page 83). If you choose to draw your templates on the paper back of these products, you will need to use a reverse image copy for your templates. Mistyfuse fusible instructions say to draw on the fusible, but the product is delicate and can be hard to draw on with accuracy. For Mistyfuse, use the Raw Edge Cut-and-Glue Template technique described on page 54. Refer to Templates and Placement Guides on page 20 for specific details on copying the patterns.

RAW EDGES

In raw edge appliqué, shapes are often cut following the edges of the paper template. The order of appliqué piecing is worked from the back shapes to the front. The patterns here are numbered to follow this order. Where one appliqué piece is overlapped by an adjoining piece, it is necessary to add seam allowances to the bottom piece to eliminate gaps between the shapes. If the fabric is dark, cut the shape by adding ⅛″ seam allowance along the edges that will be overlapped. If the fabric is light, cut the seam allowance more generously. Any edges that are not overlapped are cut following the lines on the paper template.

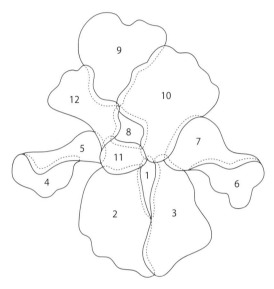

Determine seam allowances.

I apply fusible web to all my fabrics before cutting out the appliqué shapes. Follow the manufacturer's directions to adhere fusible web to the back side of the fabric. Coat the back of the template shape with Scotch Restickable Glue Stick and place the piece on the right side of the fusible web–backed appliqué fabric. The restickable glue should adhere and pull off without leaving adhesive on the fabric. Cut out each shape, adding a small seam allowance in the areas that must overlap. It's simpler than it sounds.

Fuse the shapes to the background following the manufacturer's directions. After fusing, mistakes can be peeled off from the background fabric (if the bond is poor) or a new piece can be fused over the mistake. I made *New Growth* with Lite Steam-a-Seam 2. It worked well as an adhesive, but this temporary adhesive was very temporary. It did not last over the months it took to position everything to my liking. I used pins to help it stay in place. When using other fusible products, such as 606 Spray and Fix and Bo-Nash, cut out the fabric shape, add the adhesive spray or powder to the back of the shape, and press to fuse it to the background.

New Growth by Laurel Anderson, 41″ × 47″
Fused with Lite Steam-a-Seam 2.

Fusible products can adhere to irons and pads. To protect your tools, invest in two good appliqué pressing sheets. Most are made from silicon or Polylon and are heat resistant. Choose ones that you can see through. You will want one under your work and one above. There are several products that will clean the fusible adhesive off your iron if you goof up, but it's easier to prevent the problem than to fix it.

Here's the cool thing about the pressing sheets: Because the fusibles won't permanently adhere to the sheets, you can prelayer all of your fused-appliqué pieces together on the sheet, iron them together, and then remove and reposition them to the background fabric. This is really handy if you're working with very intricate pieces of fused appliqué. These sheets are also good as table covers for glue guns and heated embellishment tools used with hot-fix crystals.

THREAD

Because the appliqué stitches will show on the finished quilt of a raw edge design, the type and color of thread you select becomes an important design element for your overall project. For instance, a perfectly matched thread will blend into the appliqué piece, creating a "calmer" look for the overall appliqué. A slightly lighter or darker thread will subtly highlight the piece. A thread that has great contrast or is a completely different color will add drama and emphasis to the appliqué piece. And, with the huge selection of metallics, variegated, and shiny specialty threads on the market, you can really have fun embellishing your appliqué while also securing the edges.

EDGE STITCHING

The edges of your fusible appliqué will lift and fray over time and use, depending on how much handling and washing is done to it. Because of this, the project can be finished with decorative edge stitching. The most common stitches used for fusible appliqué projects are the straight stitch, satin stitch, and blanket stitch.

Straight Stitch

My favorite treatment of raw edges is free-motion quilting, which is a straight stitch directed in whatever direction you wish it to go. Generally, when you free-motion quilt on your machine, you will be lowering (or dropping) your feed dogs to enable the quilt to move freely under the needle. Also, your machine probably has a special foot called a darning or free-motion foot, which rests slightly above the fabric while the stitching occurs. Stitch along the inside edges of the appliqué pieces. This secures the edges so they will withstand gentle washing. You can also free-motion stitch inside the appliqué pieces to add detail, texture, and drama to the pieces. This can be tons of fun and can really add spark and life to your overall project.

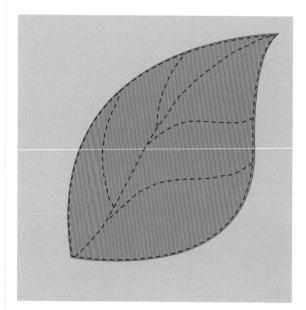

Straight stitch example

Satin Stitch

A satin stitch is really just a very tight zigzag stitch. Most machines let you control how wide or narrow the overall stitch is. Generally, you want a wider stitch for larger appliqué pieces and a narrower stitch for the smaller pieces. But, you always want to make sure that the stitch completely covers the raw edges of the appliqué piece.

With a satin stitch, because the stitch becomes a prominent design element, think carefully about the threads you choose. The satin stitch is also the stitch most resistant to fraying. But it can distort the fabric along the bias. Test the stitch on scraps that include the same fusible and fabric you're using, and choose the machine settings that distort the fabric the least. Your tension settings are very important to successful satin stitching. If your tension is too tight, the appliqué piece, and the overall project, will pucker. If it's too loose, you'll see bobbin threads on the front, or the stitches will just be very loose. Adjust your tension in very small increments, no more than a quarter step between numbers at one time. Depending on your machine and how sensitive it is to the adjustments, you might be able to find the correct setting with just a slight turn. When you do discover the needed settings for the correct tension on that particular fusible, write it down so you can refer back to it again and again.

When you're stitching your satin stitches, narrow the stitches as you reach an appliqué piece's point. Increase them again when you sew past the point. Many embroidery stitches are variations of the satin stitch. Test them before using.

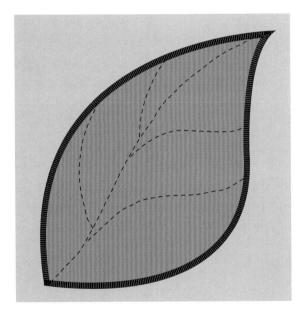

Satin stitch example

Blanket Stitch

The blanket stitch is commonly seen in quilts with a country flair. It gives a vintage look to a quilt and can also be done with machine or by hand. But, of course, the machine will be much faster.

Like the satin stitch, the blanket stitch creates a secure edge that retards fraying. And like the satin stitch, you'll need to find your correct tension for it to look good.

Generally, because the blanket stitch is a decorative stitch, most quilters choose a contrasting thread color to highlight the stitch. But, this is your choice.

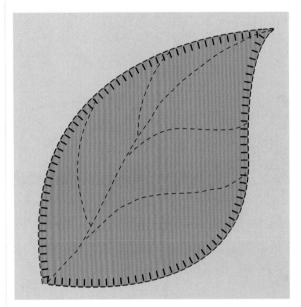

Blanket stitch example

Drafting Raw Edge Appliqué Designs

Raw edge quilt designs are the easiest to draw. There are very few rules to follow. But there are some problems with the technique that you will need to understand first. Raw edge designs fray when the quilt is washed. This is fine if you want a ragged look, which some designs welcome. However, if you're making a baby quilt or other type of quilt that will be washed often, consider using a satin stitch to secure all the edges.

Keep the edge treatments in mind when you draw your designs. You may choose to leave stitching until the quilting stage, and then add detailing to each leaf and petal. Plan on stitching slightly inside each appliqué piece's edge to secure the piece to the background. A satin stitch makes a more secure edge but leaves a wider line. Use this wider line as a design element.

With stems, satin stitch one side of the stem with dark thread to create a shadow. On the opposite edge, satin stitch with a pale, shiny thread to give an illusion of roundness. On a leaf, satin stitch beyond the lower tip to create a stem. Increase the width of the stitches to mimic a real stem. In *Autumn Breeze*, scalloped embroidery stitches were used to edge the Japanese maple leaf. The scallops gave the leaf lifelike edging. Keep in mind that the narrow stems cut on the straight of the grain will unravel faster than stems cut on the bias. Be careful not to stretch the bias stems when you glue them down.

Japanese Maple; detail of *Autumn Breeze*, page 9, by Laurel Anderson

Another consideration in designing your quilt is that multiple layers of fused fabrics add stiffness and increase the difficulty of quilting. This stiffness created with fusible web (page 58) and *Broderie Perse* (page 61) techniques may work fine for art quilts or wallhangings, but it may not be suitable for a bed quilt. School glue, used in the Cut-and-Glue method (page 54), eliminates the stiff layers but can show through to the front of the fabric. Rinsing the finished quilt in water will dissolve the glue, giving the quilt a soft hand.

Why would you even bother with raw edge designs? The benefits are that any design can be appliquéd using the raw edge methods presented in this book. Circles, stems, sharp points, and sharp V points are easy to accomplish with a good pair of scissors. Scrappy quilts, like the background of the *Stargazer Lily* (page 53) are easy, but so is a wholecloth background like in *New Growth* (page 49).

Stargazer Lily by Laurel Anderson, 17″ × 38″

Cut-and-glue appliqué

Raw Edge Cut-and-Glue Appliqué

If you love the look of appliqué but are convinced that you could never do it, try the Cut-and-Glue method. It requires the skills a first grader possesses. No, I'm not saying you have the skills of a first grader—only that your first grader can do it with you. The tools you will need are scissors, glue, and tape. Mistakes are fixed by spraying the area with water, waiting until the glue dissolves, and lifting the shape off the background. Machine quilting may be more difficult because the glue does not always hold the edges securely.

The project for this technique is presented in two parts. The first part of the project is assembling the background panel using the Turned Edge Quick Appliqué method (page 33). In this chapter, I will demonstrate how to construct the iris flower for this quilt. This quick and simple technique works well for any appliqué shapes. The glue is washed out after assembly, so prewashing fabrics is recommended for colorfastness. Do not use this method for fabrics that bleed color.

PRACTICE:
Raw Edge Cut-and-Glue Appliqué
IRIS PANEL QUILT

FINISHED SIZE: 9″ × 21″

Fire Iris by Laurel Anderson

Supplies

- Fabrics (see Turned Edge Quick Appliqué, page 33)

- Plain copy paper, 8½" × 11"

- Scissors for paper and fabric

- Scotch Restickable Glue Stick

- Plastic wrap

- School glue or Roxanne Glue-Baste-It

- Scotch tape

Preparing the Pattern Pieces

1. Use a pencil and lightbox or window to trace 2 copies of the Iris Flower template (pullout P1) on plain paper. One copy will be used as a placement guide and the other as appliqué templates. Include numbers on both copies. Each piece is numbered and will be appliquéd in order.

2. Mark a seam allowance along overlapping edges (see Raw Edges, page 49). A red pen or pencil works well to mark the seam allowance. If the fabric is dark, mark ¼" seam allowance. If the fabric is light in color, draw the seam allowance to give the look of petals overlapping.

3. Spread restickable glue on the back side of the uncut traced appliqué template. Allow the glue to dry for about a minute.

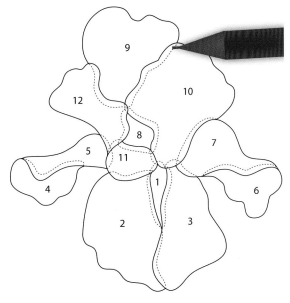

Mark seam allowances for overlapped edges.

Putting It Together

1. Assemble the appliqué background panel, including the leaves and stem, following Turned Edge Quick Appliqué, page 33.

2. Cut out the entire Flower template as one piece along the outer edges of the drawn lines.

> If the flower is a pale color and will be placed over a dark background, cut the shape of the full flower from a layer of white fabric. Position the shape on the placement guide, and assemble the flower pieces on top. This will filter the dark background fabric from showing through light petals.

3. Cut out petal 1 from the paper template; cut along the lines and include the added seam allowance.

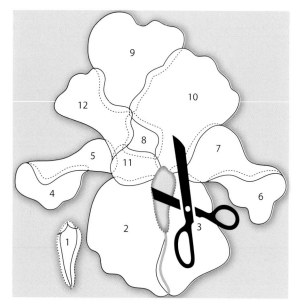

Iris template with seam allowances marked

4. Stick the template shape to the front side of the iris fabric (the restickable glue should adhere and pull off without leaving adhesive on the fabric).

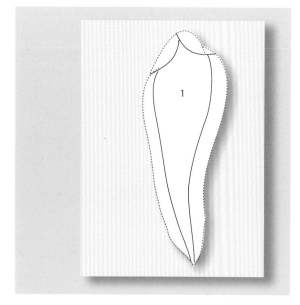

Stick pattern piece onto right side of fabric.

5. Cut out the fabric along the edge of the paper template shape. Gently peel the paper template off the fabric and lay the fabric shape in place on the placement guide.

> Put a layer of plastic wrap over the placement guide to prevent it from getting damaged.

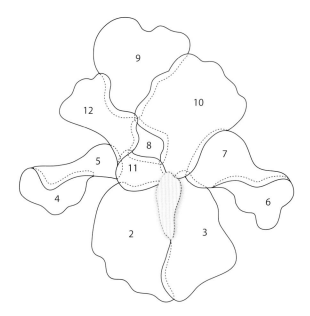

Place the fabric shape on the placement guide.

6. Tape the paper shape back in place on the paper iris pattern.

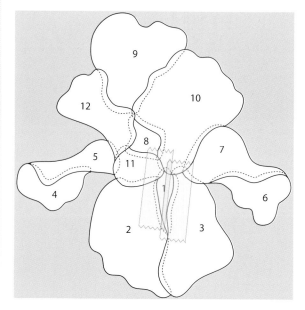

Tape the template back together.

7. Cut out petal piece 2 from the paper template, remembering to include the seam allowance at overlapping edges. Place the template on the front of the fabric, as in Step 4, and cut along the edge of the template.

8. Place small dots of school glue or Glue-Baste-It along the adjoining seam allowance of piece 1. Use a minimum of glue; it just needs to hold the fabrics together until they are stitched.

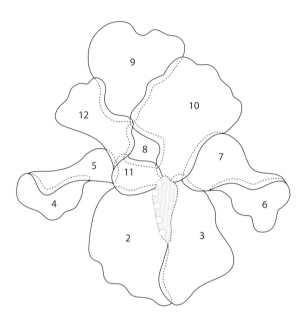

9. Gently peel off the paper template of piece 2 and lay the fabric shape in place on the placement guide.

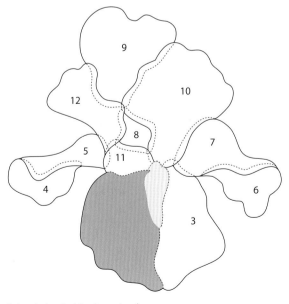

School glue holds pieces in place.

10. Tape the paper pattern back together. Cut out each remaining petal in numbered order and glue it in place on the placement guide. Tape the pattern back together after each petal is placed.

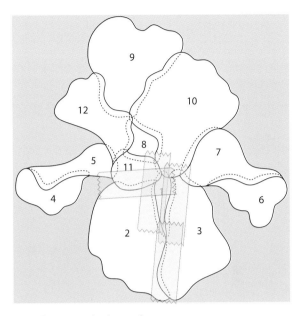

Tape the pattern back together.

11. When all the petals are cut out and assembled on the placement guide, stand back and evaluate the design. If a piece needs replacing, spray the adjoining glue dots with water. Allow the water to soften the glue for a few minutes and then gently separate the pieces. Cut a new piece and glue in place.

12. Place the assembled appliqué unit on the background panel. Glue the unit in place with small dots of school glue or Glue-Baste-It. The iris will be stitched during the final quilting of the quilt sandwich.

13. See Finishing the Quilt, page 36, for directions on completing the Iris Panel Quilt.

Raw Edge Appliqué Using Fusible Web

Fusible appliqué has many fans. Quite a few nationally acclaimed quilters use fusibles for all of their appliqué projects. I especially like to use fusible appliqué when I have a beautiful background fabric. The fusible retards fraying of the fabric edges. The stiffness that the fusible web adds to the fabric helps stabilize the appliqué pieces for satin stitching or other edge finishing.

A wide variety of fusible products are on the market. For a comparison of these products see Fusible Product Comparison Chart on page 83. For all fusible products, the heat of the iron melts the adhesive and creates a bond between the fabrics in the appliqué pieces and the background. This creates a raw edge appliqué that you may or may not choose to stitch down at the project's end. Generally, the fusible will loosen over time with washing and wear. Also, the finished project's look can be greatly enhanced by the stitching used on the raw edges. If you can invest in the time, stitching these edges will probably work best for your project, and you can even experiment with those glorious specialty threads teasing you in your local quilt shop! To finish the edges of the fusible appliqué, stitch along the edges using a satin stitch, straight stitch, buttonhole stitch, or any other stitching you'd like (see Edge Stitching, page 50).

With this project, the raw edge appliqué flowers, stems, and leaves are added with fusible web after the cameo-style background is completed. The leaves overflow out of the oval opening.

PRACTICE:
Raw Edge Appliqué Using Fusible Web

CALLA LILY TRIO

FINISHED SIZE: 17½″ × 23¼″

Calla Lily Trio **by Laurel Anderson**

Supplies

Choose fabrics that provide contrast between background and flowers. Prewash and press all fabrics. Hand-dyed or batik fabrics can provide deep, rich color variations (see Hand Dyeing Your Own Fabric, page 89).

- 10" × 10" square fabric for outer calla flowers
- 6" × 6" square pale fabric for calla edges
- 10" × 10" square medium fabric for inner calla flowers
- 4" × 4" square fabric for spadix (spikes of flower)
- 1 fat quarter each of 2 fabrics for leaves
- 4" × 10" rectangle each of 3 fabrics for stems and folds of leaves
- ¾ yard fabric for background, cut to 19" × 25"
- ¾ yard fabric for cameo border facing, cut to 19" × 25"
- ⅓ yard fabric for detail strip
- ¾ yard fabric for backing
- Batting, 20" × 26"
- 1 yard fusible web
- Tracing paper, or newsprint, for facing template
- Plain copy paper, 11" × 17" or larger
- Scissors for paper and for fabric
- Scotch Restickable Glue Stick
- 2 appliqué transparent pressing sheets, silicone sheets, or parchment paper
- Iron and pad

Preparing the Pattern Pieces

1. Trace 1 copy of the background oval opening and curved borders of the Calla Lily Trio Facing Template (pullout P3) onto tracing paper.

2. Use a pencil and lightbox or window to trace 1 copy of the center floral arrangement and oval opening on plain paper to use as a placement guide. Include numbers on the copy.

3. Using the same method, trace 1 copy of the flowers, leaves, and stems on plain paper. Use this copy for appliqué templates. Include numbers in the copy. Note that each piece is numbered and will be appliquéd in order. Pencil in ⅛" overlap seam allowances for adjoining shapes (see Raw Edges, page 49).

4. Spread restickable glue on the backside of the uncut traced appliqué templates. Allow the glue to dry for about a minute.

> OPTIONAL METHOD: Some fusible web products have a paper backing. For these products the template shapes can be traced, with a lightbox or window, directly onto the paper backing in mirror image (reverse). The paper-backed fusible web is then fused to the *wrong* side of the appliqué fabric. Shapes are cut following the traced lines, and the paper backing is removed before fusing to the background.

Putting It Together

1. Create the cameo background following Completing a Quilt with a Facing on page 84. This makes a completed quilt on which to fuse the flowers and leaves.

2. Cut the flowers, stems, and leaves out of the template paper.

3. Follow the manufacturer's directions for the fusible web to fuse the webbing to the wrong side of the appliqué fabrics. Before fusing, protect your iron and pad by placing an appliqué pressing sheet underneath and on top of the layered fabric.

4. Lay each paper template shape on top of the fused fabric. Cut out the fabric shapes along the template lines. Remove any fusible paper backing. Cut around templates, adding extra seam allowances for petal overlap (see Raw Edges, page 49).

5. Place the placement guide on the iron pad and cover it with a pressing sheet. Use the placement guide to arrange the flowers and leaves on the pressing sheet. Remove the paper templates. Cover the pieces with a pressing sheet, being careful not to disturb the placement. Fuse each layered flower and leaf as a separate appliqué unit.

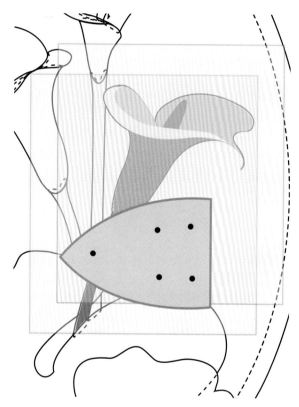

Fuse layers to create appliqué units.

6. Position the placement guide on the completed cameo background. Arrange the stems and flower units in their correct position. Carefully remove the placement guide. Fuse the callas and stems to the background.

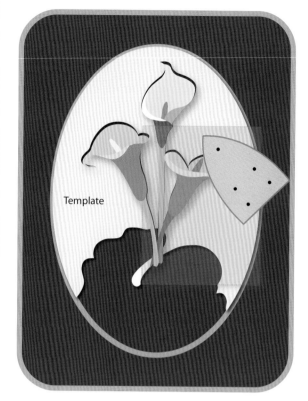

Template

Fuse stems and flowers to background.

7. Reposition the placement guide on the background, arranging the leaves over the stems and facing. Carefully remove the placement guide and fuse in place.

Finishing the Quilt

1. Finish the edges of the fused pieces using a satin stitch, straight stitch, buttonhole stitch, or any other stitching you'd like. These stitches are explained on pages 50–51.

2. Quilt the finished top as desired.

Raw Edge Three-Dimensional *Broderie Perse* Appliqué

Broderie Perse is a fancy French name for a very simple technique. *Broderie Perse* is an old technique originally used to sew chintz fabric flowers onto muslin. In the traditional method, a motif shape is cut from the printed fabric and stitched down, leaving the edges raw. For this project I offer a modern version using *Broderie Perse* with your sewing machine to create three-dimensional petals and leaves.

Three-dimensional appliqué can be fun with this modified *Broderie Perse* method. Using a fusible product that is fairly firm, two fabrics are fused together, wrong sides facing. The three-dimensional unit is then stitched into place, allowing some parts to remain unattached. If you will be sending your quilt out to be quilted, add these three-dimensional elements after the quilting is complete.

This project shows the technique for creating petals and leaves that hang below the oval cameo border. For more information about selecting a fusible product for this project, see Fusible Product Comparison Chart on page 83.

PRACTICE:
Raw Edge Three-Dimensional *Broderie Perse* Appliqué
CONEFLOWER

FINISHED SIZE: 17″ × 22″

Coneflower by Mary Wilkinson, pattern by Laurel Anderson

Supplies

Choose fabrics that provide contrast between background and flowers. Hand-dyed fabrics can provide deep, rich color variations. Consider using them instead of commercial fabrics (see Hand Dyeing Your Own Fabric, page 89).

- ⅓ yard fabrics for petals
- 6″ × 6″ square fabric for flower center
- 8″ × 8″ square each of 4 fabrics for leaves
- 6″ × 16″ fabric for stems
- ¾ yard fabric for background, cut to 18″ × 24″
- ¾ yard fabric for cameo border facing, cut to 18″ × 24″
- ⅓ yard fabric for inner detail strip
- ⅓ yard fabric for outer detail strip
- ¾ yard fabric for backing
- Batting, 19″ × 24″
- 1 yard fusible web
- Tracing paper, or newsprint, for facing template
- Plain copy paper, 11″ × 17″ or larger
- Scissors for paper and for fabric
- Scotch Restickable Glue Stick
- 2 appliqué transparent pressing sheets, silicone sheets, or parchment paper
- Iron and pad

Preparing the Pattern Pieces

1. Trace on tracing paper 1 copy of the background oval opening and curved borders of the *Calla Lily Trio* facing template (pullout P3).

2. Use a pencil and lightbox or window to trace 1 copy of the center floral arrangement and oval opening on plain paper. Include numbers on the copy. Use this copy as the placement guide.

3. Use the same method to trace 1 copy each of the flowers, leaves, and stems on plain paper (pullout P3 and P4). Use these copies as appliqué templates. Include numbers on the copies. Note that each piece is numbered and will be appliquéd in order.

4. Spread restickable glue on the back side of the uncut traced appliqué templates. Allow the glue to dry for about a minute.

Putting It Together

1. Use the placement guide to position and appliqué the stems, flower centers, and inner leaves to the background fabric with Raw Edge Appliqué Using Fusible Web (page 58) or Needle-Turn Hand Appliqué (page 67).

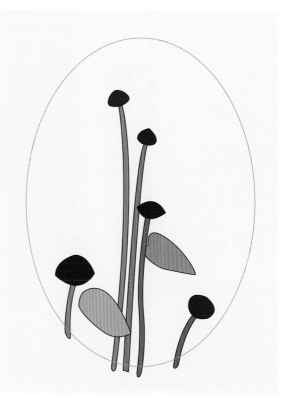

Appliqué stems, flower center, and inner leaves.

2. To make 3-dimensional petals and leaves, follow the manufacturer's directions for the fusible web and fuse the webbing to the *wrong* side of 3 petal fabrics. Before fusing, protect your iron and pad by placing an appliqué pressing sheet underneath and on top of the layered fabric. Remove paper backing, if necessary.

3. Place a second layer of petal fabric over the fused webbing, wrong side facing the web. Fuse the layers together, creating three 2-sided petal fabrics.

4. In the same manner, fuse 2 layers of leaf fabric, creating two 2-sided leaf fabrics.

5. Lay each leaf and petal paper template shape on top of its corresponding 2-sided fabric. Cut out the shapes along the template lines. Leave the paper template on the pieces, except while finishing the edges. The numbered templates will serve as a label when stitching the pieces to the quilt. Satin or blanket stitch the edges to finish each, if desired.

Finishing the Quilt

1. Use the appliquéd background to assemble the cameo facing, using the directions in Traditional Facing Technique with Detail Strip on page 85.

2. Quilt as desired.

3. Use the placement guide to position the 2-sided petals and leaves on the background. Remove the template paper and attach each petal and leaf to the front of the quilt, sewing down the center of each. Pieces should be three-dimensional and unattached along the side edges.

Sew down center of flowers and leaves to attach.

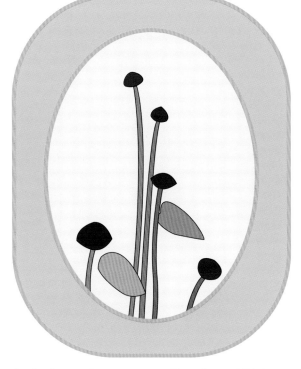

Appliqué stems, flower centers, and inner leaves visible in oval opening of facing.

Classic Needle-Turn Hand Appliqué

Hand appliqué is the gold standard of all the methods. It's portable, traditional, and gives the stitched shapes a bit of loft. Hand appliqué works best for shapes without sharp, narrow corners. It's also the method with the simplest tools.

Appliqué liberates the quilt designer from the regimentation of geometric designs. It enhances freedom of expression. Throughout the centuries of quilting, appliqué elevated quilts from humble to grand works of art. I have noticed that quilt shows award more ribbons to appliqué quilts. You don't want to miss your share of blue ribbons.

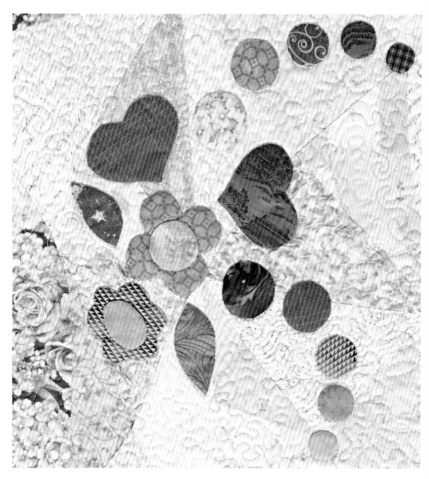

Hand-appliquéd flowers. Detail of *Inherit the Love*, page 76.

If you have never hand appliquéd before, you may wonder why anyone would love it. Those of you who do love hand appliqué are now shouting at this book. There is a Zen-like feeling that comes over you when you hand appliqué, especially when you're relaxed and taking your time. One of the nicest things is the portability of your projects. You can hand appliqué anywhere: in an airport, in court, in a doctor's office, or in a covered wagon.

Up until late in the twentieth century, appliqué was always done by hand. The wealth of appliqué styles and patterns are predominantly designed for handwork. It's only during the past fifteen years that a growth of patterns designed for other appliqué methods has become available.

Although I have presented the turned edge chapters as machine appliqué techniques, it is interesting to note that all of them can be adapted to use hand stitching instead of the machine (see Appliqué Ratings Chart, page 17). Hand appliqué has many refinements of method. In this chapter, we'll explore classic needle-turn appliqué; however, you may find that other variations of hand appliqué are easier for you.

Visit my website, www.whispercolor.com, to find links to various hand appliqué resources.

Drafting
Hand Appliqué Designs

Coneflowers by Laurel Anderson, 17″ × 22″

Many Best-of-Show quilts are hand appliquéd. Can you blame the judges? After all, a beautifully crafted, hand-appliquéd quilt is something I stop and look at with wonder and awe when I visit quilt shows. I have friends who can do anything with hand appliqué, but most of us don't have enough practice to make ⅛-inch stems or blueberry-sized circles. But, with practice, you can get there as well. Start with something easy and build your skills. Sharp points are difficult, so start by drawing patterns with slight curves. Tight curves are difficult, so draw the curves gently.

Let the fabric provide some of the design. Large prints often have color transitions that can be used instead of an additional piece of fabric. The same is true for hand-dyed or batik fabrics; their color and value transitions can imitate colors found in nature. Instead of appliquéing three different fabrics to show the color change in a flower, consider using one hand-dyed fabric that contains all the colors needed. To make your own hand-dyed fabrics, refer to Hand Dyeing Your Own Fabric on page 89.

Consider using freezer paper or plain paper templates when constructing the design. Freezer paper can be used on the top or back of the appliqué fabric. The paper templates hold the shapes together during the stitching process and provide stability to the fabric during hand appliqué. The paper templates are removed after the appliqué work is complete, producing a soft hand in the finished design. Refer to the Turned Edge Machine Appliqué chapters (pages 19–47) for guidance in using paper templates during construction.

Keep practicing your techniques. Remember that Baltimore Album quilts are not made in a day and that you will improve with time.

Hand Appliqué Tool Kit

The following is a basic tool kit for performing hand appliqué. There are so many brands and types of tools on the market today that I'm not recommending any particular brand. Feel free to test what's out there until you find what works best for you. Better yet, get with your stitching pals and see what they're using.

TEMPLATES

Any good paper will make a template. Instead of pins to hold the templates in place, use Scotch Restickable Glue Stick (page 29) on the back of the paper. This low-tack adhesive will not leave a residue. Freezer paper templates, with their waxy backing, can be temporarily fused to the fabric. Choose copy paper or freezer paper for shapes to be used once.

For more durability, choose card stock or cereal boxes to make templates. The edges of these heavier papers will eventually distort with repeated use. When making many identical shapes, invest in some good heat-resistant template plastic and cut your shapes knowing they will last.

MECHANICAL PENCIL

Mechanical pencils tend to leave the smallest line on the fabric. Purchase extra lead. Use white pencils for marking on dark fabric.

NEEDLES

Every experienced quilter has a favorite appliqué needle. Try several until you find your favorite. Needles with rough or small eyes tend to shred the thread. Choices include sharps, quilters, and milliners. But again, this is a very personal decision made by each quilter. When you find what works, stock up.

THIMBLE

It is amazing how many styles of thimbles are available. Thimbles limit, but don't eliminate, bleeding onto quilts. They protect the tips of your fingers from the constant pricking of the needle. It's important to find what will work best for you.

PINS

I like the thin, expensive kind with flat heads. But again, pins come in all shapes and sizes. Some appliquérs swear by the small, silk pins, which they use to hold tiny pieces of appliqué in place. Another popular type for larger areas is the extra-long, thin pins with glass heads. Again, find what works and stick with it, but a couple of different lengths might be what fills your arsenal.

THREAD

The most important thing to remember about thread is to match its color to the piece being appliquéd. This is especially true when stitches need to be invisible, as in hand appliqué or some of the machine appliqué techniques.

I'm going to break away here and recommend my favorite threads, which are Masterpiece, Bottom Line, or So Fine, all from Superior Threads. They are thin and strong. I admit to using any thread that matches, even from my vintage collection. YLI Silk and YLI SoftTouch also work well. Some threads shred easily. If this happens, change your needle or use a different thread. Sometimes 100 percent polyester thread behaves the best for tightly woven fabric such as batiks.

SCISSORS

I use small, sharp-pointed scissors with cushioned handles. Fiskars Softgrip or Ginghers serrated edge scissors are two good brands. But, again, there are many others out there. Find what works for you.

PRACTICE:
Needle-Turn Hand Appliqué

Rather than providing a complete project to demonstrate needle-turn appliqué, I'm showing the techniques needed to approach various shapes. Use these techniques to adapt any of the templates provided in the pullouts to create a hand appliqué quilt. I hand appliquéd the flower centers and stems of the *Coneflower* (page 61) quilt.

Supplies

- Various fabrics, small scraps

- See Hand Appliqué Tool Kit (page 66)

PREPARING THE PATTERN PIECES

Trace pattern onto template material. Cut out template.

NEEDLE-TURN HAND APPLIQUÉ TECHNIQUES

Hand Appliqué Basics

1. Using a sharp pencil or chalk pencil, trace the shape onto the right side of both the appliqué and background fabrics.

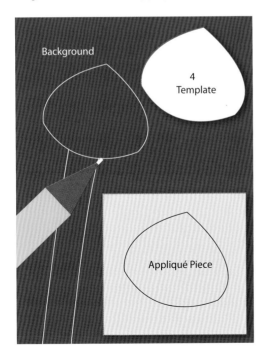

Trace shape onto fabric.

2. Cut out the appliqué shape, adding a ⅛" seam allowance.

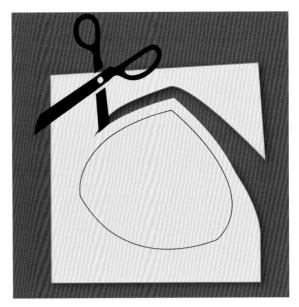

Cut out appliqué piece with a ⅛" seam allowance.

3. Pin the shape in place on the background fabric. Use the needle to turn under the seam allowance until the pencil mark is slightly under the shape. Knot the thread and come up from the background, catching a few threads of the shape along the fold. Return the needle back through the stitch in the background fabric.

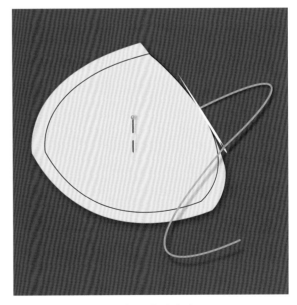

Turn seam allowance under and stitch down.

4. Continue stitching, using small and even stitches, bringing the needle up through the background, and catching a few threads of the fabric fold. Pull thread firmly. Return your needle through the hole in the background and repeat. Stitch evenly, pulling the thread tight so it will hide in the fabric.

5. Clip the seam allowance in all inner (concave) curves and inner points.

Hand Appliquéing Outer Points

1. Take several small stitches before reaching the outer point. These stitches will help accentuate the point.

2. Clip the point, leaving the smallest seam allowance, and turn under.

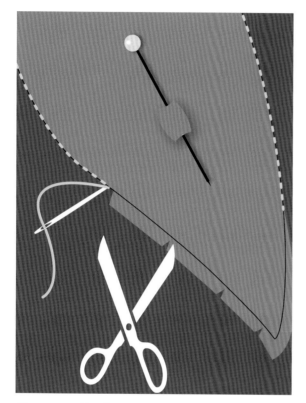

Clip curves and inside points.

Clip corner off.

3. Stitch, using very small stitches, until you sew past the point, adding one stitch at the point to secure it down.

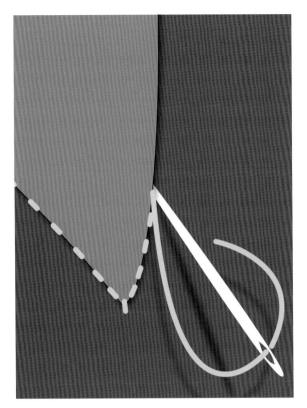

Stitch past point.

Hand Appliquéing Inner Points

1. Clip the inner points just before reaching them.

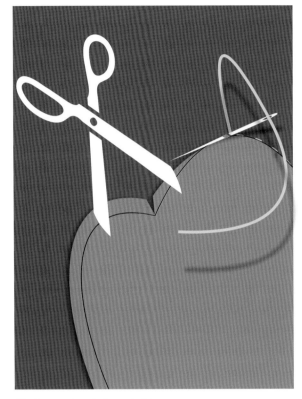

Clip inner points before stitching.

2. Stitch small stitches on either side of them to secure any loose threads.

Hand Appliquéing Circles

1. Choose a firm template material such as heat-resistant template plastic, card stock, or two layers of freezer paper.

2. Cut appliqué fabric ⅜" larger than the template.

Leave ⅜" seam allowance.

3. Sew a running stitch, using strong thread, ¼" beyond the edge of the template. Pull stitches tight to gather fabric. Adjust gathers to give a smooth edge. Press using starch.

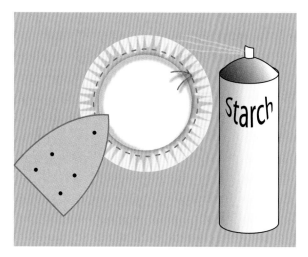

Gently pull thread to draw in circle's edges.

4. Position the circle on the background and appliqué in place using the basic stitch (see Hand Appliqué Basics, page 67).

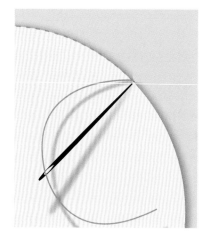

Appliqué circle to background.

5. Trim away the background fabric behind the circle allowing a ¼" seam allowance. Remove the template.

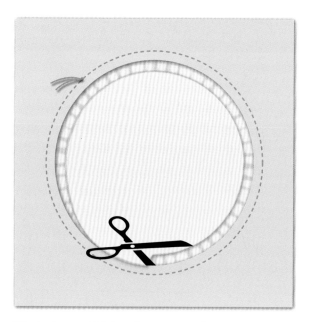

Trim background fabric and remove template.

Appliquéing Stems

1. Cut bias strips from stem fabric. Use a square of fabric and cut the strips from corner to opposite corner, cutting the strips double the desired width plus ½". Cut strips the length needed plus ½".

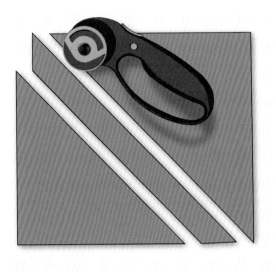

Cut bias strips.

2. Create a hem on any ends that will show on the finished piece. Fold under ¼" on each end and press. Trim the folded hem to ⅛".

3. Fold the stem fabric in half lengthwise, wrong sides together.

4. Measure from the fold, and mark the desired finished stem width. Pin the marked line to the right stem line on the background. Make sure the stem fold faces away from the stem.

5. Stitch through the mark and background by hand or machine. Trim the seam allowance to ⅛".

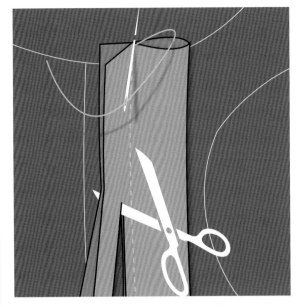

Stitch to right stem mark and trim seam to ⅛".

6. Rotate the stitched tube so the fold meets the left stem mark on the background.

7. Appliqué the stem to the background fabric along the left stem marking.

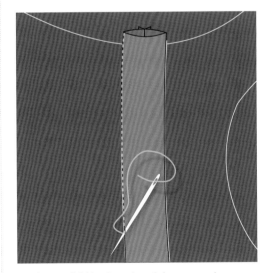

Stitch stem fold in place along left stem mark.

Gallery

BLUE IRIS CAMEO by Laurel Anderson, 22" × 31"

PURPLE IRIS by Laurel Anderson, 9″ × 22″

INDIAN SUMMER TULIP by Laurel Anderson, 9″ × 22″

KING EDWARD TULIP by Laurel Anderson, 9″ × 22″

FIRST LADY TULIP, by Laurel Anderson, 9″ x 22″

PURPLE MOUNT DIABLO by Laurel Anderson, 18″ × 15″

TIDINGS OF GREAT JOY by Laurel Anderson, 39″ × 51″

INHERIT THE LOVE by Laurel Anderson, 40″ × 52″

WHISPER OF SPRING by Laurel Anderson, 72″ × 18″

END OF WINTER by Laurel Anderson, 18″ × 18″

TULIP TANGO by Laurel Anderson, 18″ × 18″

THE STORY OF LIFE by Laurel Anderson, 34" × 39"

POINSETTIA AND VASE by Laurel Anderson, 34" × 49"

Poinsettia pattern by Phil Beaver

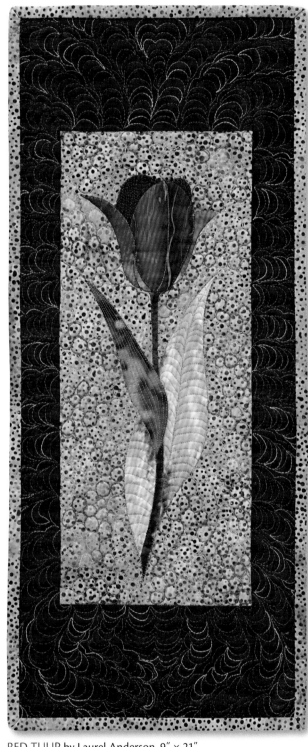

RED TULIP by Laurel Anderson, 9″ × 21″

MAGNOLIA BUD by Laurel Anderson, 8″ × 8″

CHARLOTTE'S CHINA CABINET by Laurel Anderson, 53" × 53"

IRIS CAMEO COAT, quilted by Sherry Werum

Turned edge and raw edge appliqué with vintage lace and brocades

IRIS CAMEO COAT, quilted by Sherry Werum

FIRST BLUSH by Laurel Anderson, 49″ × 49″

FRESH BREEZE by Laurel Anderson, 86″ × 28″

Fusible Product Comparison Chart

In this book I've provided several techniques for fusible appliqué. From fusible webs to sprays and powders, a wide variety of products are available for use in appliqué. To help you decide what works best for your needs, I've provided you with a comparison chart of some of the most popular fusible products on the market. The chart shows the differences between the products, the techniques required for appliqué, and the final look and feel of the finished design. It's important to understand these differences when selecting a product to work with. For example, some fusible webs like Steam-A-Seam 2 come with paper backing, while others like Mistyfuse don't have any backing. The presence

or absence of the paper backing dictates where you'll draw your pattern shapes.

In this chart, I've included information about pattern reversing and where to draw the pattern shapes. Although I've included pressing instructions for each product, you should always refer to the manufacturer's directions. Some fusibles love steam; others, dry heat. Still others like high temperatures, and then there are delicate fusibles that will melt into nothing with high temperatures. The chart's ratings of "Soft Hand" were rated by my family members. When you try different fusible products, be sure to rate them for yourself and add your notes to the chart.

Fusible Product	Pattern Reversing Required	Where to Draw Pattern Shapes	Iron Temperature	Ironing Time	Soft Hand (1 = soft to 5 = firm)
Steam-A-Seam 2 Lite fusible web	Yes	Paper backing side that is harder to remove	Cotton setting, Dry	10–15 seconds; longer with pressing sheet	3
Wonder-Under fusible web	Yes	Paper backing	Wool setting, Dry	5–8 seconds to back of patch; 10–15 seconds onto background if covered with damp pressing cloth	2
HeatnBond Lite fusible web	Yes	Paper backing	Silk setting, Dry	2 seconds to back of patch; 8–10 seconds onto background	4
Mistyfuse fusible web	No	Fusible or fabric	Cotton or setting appropriate for fabric	5–15 seconds with Teflon pressing sheet or parchment paper	1
Stitch Witchery fusible web	No	Fabric	Wool, Dry	10 seconds over a damp pressing cloth	5
606 Spray and Fix fusible adhesive	No	Fabric (see page 37 for use with freezer paper)	Cotton, Dry	30–45 seconds; use parchment paper and moving iron	4
Bo-Nash Bonding Agent fusible powder	No	Fabric	Cotton, Dry	2–3 seconds, depending on thickness of fabric	5

Completing a Quilt with a Facing

I frequently use shaped facings for my quilts. Facings are pieces of fabric used to finish raw edges around an opening. In the garment industry, facings are used in shirts around necklines or armholes. For quilters, facings can be used to finish a quilt while at the same time adding unique design elements, such as curved outer borders or cameo-style framing. Facings are wonderful choices for quilts with curved corners.

Shaped facings can be made with or without interfacing. In *Iris Cameo*, I used the Traditional Facing Technique with Detail Strip (page 85) to add a design element to the quilt. This technique creates a finished edge along the center opening and outer edge of the quilt. No hand work or additional binding is needed. This cameo-style opening frames my appliquéd center.

Iris Cameo by Laurel Anderson, 22″ × 31″

In *Dogwood* (page 37), I used the Faux Facing Technique for Borders (page 88) to add a curved border. This faux facing adds just the curved border, leaving the outer edge unfinished. The outer edge can later be finished with a traditional binding or pillowcase style. Wini Fung used the same technique in her modified version of *Dogwood*, adding a binding to accent her quilt.

Dogwood by Wini Fung, pattern by Laurel Anderson, 11" × 16"

Although they look complicated, these facing techniques are easy to master and produce stunning quilts. I prefer the look of the Traditional Facing Technique, but the Faux Facing Technique for Borders is a quick alternative.

Traditional Facing Technique with Detail Strip

MAKING THE DETAIL STRIP

1. Cut 1" strips of fabric on the bias. Cut enough strips to go around the center oval and outer border.

2. Stitch the bias strips together with diagonal seams by placing the right sides together and stitching across the overlap at a 45° angle. Open the seam to check for accuracy. Trim the seam allowance to ¼".

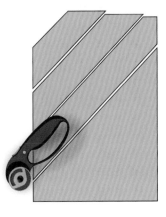

Cut strips on the bias.

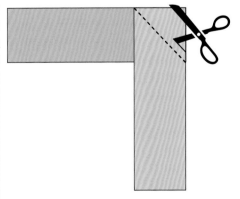

Sew strips with a diagonal seam.

3. With wrong sides together, press the strips in half lengthwise, matching raw edges. Folded strips will measure ½″ wide.

ASSEMBLING THE QUILT

1. Copy the facing template on the tracing paper or newsprint. Cut out the template along the outer curved lines and inner curved opening.

2. Place the facing fabric, right side up, on a flat surface.

3. Position the facing template on the right side of the facing fabric. Use restickable glue on the back of the template to hold it in place.

Position facing template on fabric.

4. Align the folded edge of the detail strip along the edges of the template paper, with the raw edges of the detail strip facing away from the template. Pin the strips in place around the inner curved opening and outer edges.

5. Join the meeting ends of the detail strip, overlapping the ending tail onto the beginning tail. Leaving at least a 3″ overlap, open the ending tail and trim at a 45° angle. Fold under the cut edge ¼″ and pin in place.

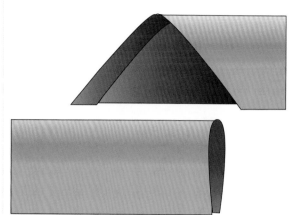

Join meeting ends of the detail strip.

6. Stitch along the detail strip ¼″ from the folded edge, removing the pins as you go.

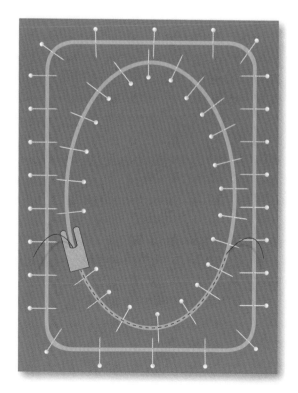

Pin detail strip in place.

7. Layer the quilt components in order on a flat surface, starting with the finished quilt top, centering and smoothing layers between each addition:

- Layer 1 (bottom layer): Quilt top, right side **down**

- Layer 2: Batting

- Layer 3: Backing fabric, right side **up**

- Layer 4 (top layer): Facing, right side **down**. Make certain the curved opening is positioned properly over the appliqué on the quilt top.

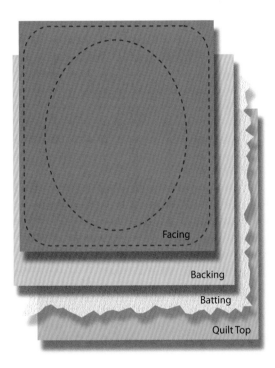

Layer quilt components.

8. Pin along the outer edges of the layered quilt to secure the layers in place.

9. Stitch along the outer edges, following the detail strip's stitching line. Sew through all layers, backstitching at the stop and start. Then, trim the seam allowance to ¼" from the stitching line, removing the excess bulk from the batting, backing, and quilt top layers.

Stitch layers together.

10. Carefully pull the facing fabric away from the quilt backing before trimming a ¼" seam allowance inside the stitching line of the curved opening. Be careful not to cut the quilt back. Clip the seam allowance along the curved opening, but not through the stitching. Clipping the curve will allow the detail strip to lie smoothly when it is turned right side out.

Trim away center opening.

11. Turn the facing to the front of the quilt, pulling on the detail strip to smooth the outer edges.

12. Turn under the raw edges of the detail strip and facing along the curved opening. Smooth the facing over the quilt. Press.

13. Pin the detail strip along the curved opening and stitch in the ditch along the seam between the detail strip and the facing.

14. Quilt as desired.

Faux Facing Technique for Borders

1. Position the facing template on the smooth side of the fusible interfacing. Use restickable glue on the back of the template to hold it in place. Trace the inner curves on the smooth side of the interfacing.

2. Place the fusible side of the interfacing face down onto the right side of the border fabric.

3. Stitch along the inner curve line.

4. Trim away the center opening along the inner curve's stitching, allowing a ¼″ seam allowance on the border fabric and a ⅛″ seam allowance on the interfacing. Clip the seam allowance along the curves.

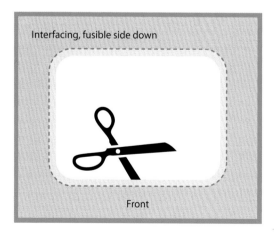

Trim seam allowances.

5. Turn the interfacing through the opening, repositioning it onto the back of the fabric, with the fusible side facing up. Finger-press the interfacing to slightly roll it under the border fabric.

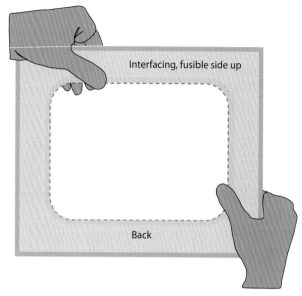

Turn border right side out.

6. Position the border frame so it is centered on the front of the quilt top, fusible side down. Press to fuse the layers, following the manufacturer's recommendations for the fusible interfacing.

7. Layer the quilt top and batting and quilt as desired, without a backing.

8. Place the facing template on the batting side of the quilted top. Trace the outer curved rectangle with a marking pencil.

9. Layer the quilted top and backing with the right sides together. Pin.

10. Stitch along the outer curved rectangle line, leaving a 5″ opening at the top.

11. Trim the quilt top seam allowance to ⅛″ and the backing seam allowance to ¼″.

12. Turn the quilt right side out. Hand stitch the opening closed. Press.

Hand Dyeing Your Own Fabric

Hand-dyed and batik fabrics have color and value transitions that can be used to imitate the colors found in nature. I use them quite often in my appliqué quilts. Instead of appliquéing three different fabrics to show the changes of color on one petal, I use a hand-dyed fabric with all the colors needed. I enjoy the process of fabric dyeing. Dyeing fabric requires careful setup and some experimentation, but the results are so wonderful that you'll be itching to use all of those new colors you've created. Check Resources (page 94) for dyeing supplies and other information. This chapter covers a few techniques to make fabrics for flower quilts.

Supplies

- Procion MX dyes in colors for leaves and flower petals
- Soda ash fixer (sodium carbonate)
- Box of plain table salt
- Glauber's salt (optional), for colors with turquoise
- Prepared-for-dyeing (PFD) fabric: fat quarters for dyeing and a larger piece for drop cloth
- Dust mask
- Rubber gloves
- Clothing and shoes that can get dye on them
- Gallon jugs such as clean, plastic, milk containers
- Small plastic containers that hold at least 1 cup fluid; 1 for each dye color you plan to use

- Plastic spoons or sticks, for mixing
- Measuring spoons, teaspoon and tablespoon size
- Measuring cup
- Funnel
- Hot water
- Spray bottle
- Gallon zip-close bags, one for each fat quarter
- Sharpie pen for labeling zip-close bags
- Retayne for setting dark colors
- Synthrapol or other good detergent for final wash
- Shout Color Catcher sheets
- Plastic sheeting for the tables and floor, if necessary

Basic Dye Information

- Combining complements on the color wheel results in gray.

- Turquoise requires hotter water to dissolve the powder, and it is best if Glauber's salt is used instead of plain salt. (See Resources, page 94, for dye chemicals.)

- Reds can be hard to dissolve. Stir the first tablespoon of water into the dye with care. Strain dye through old nylons or tights to remove undissolved grains.

- Dye colors with a * on the label require 2 tablespoons dye powder to 1 cup water for saturated colors.

- Dye colors with ** require 4 tablespoons dye powder to 1 cup water. Double the salt in the fixative mixture with these dyes.

- Soda ash is hard on fabric. Cotton stands up very well to soda ash, but rayon and silk do not. Increase the soda ash for blacks and other dark colors.

Basic Dye Recipe

Always wear a mask, gloves, and old clothing when mixing dyes.

> 1–4 tablespoons dye powder
>
> 1 cup hot tap water

While wearing gloves and mask, put the dye powder in small containers. (I do this on top of a damp drop cloth of PFD cotton.) Add 1 tablespoon of hot water and stir out all dye lumps. Add remainder of hot water slowly and stir well.

With a damp corner of the drop cloth, wipe the dye containers and measuring spoons. Before removing your mask, wet down and wipe up any dye powder that may have spilled. Reds sometimes do not completely dissolve. Strain your reds through an old pair of nylons; otherwise, the undissolved crystals will leave red spots.

Fixative Recipe

Always wear a mask, gloves, and old clothing when mixing fixative.

> ½ cup salt
>
> 4 teaspoons soda ash (may use up to ½ cup to dye dark colors)
>
> 1 gallon hot water

Combine all 3 ingredients and mix well.

Dyeing the Fabric

DYEING FABRIC FOR LEAVES

1. Soak PFD fabric in the fixative mixture for 20 minutes prior to dyeing. Wring out the fabric.

2. Roll fabric into a tube shape.

Rolled fabric

3. Put fabric roll in a zip-close bag.

4. Add just enough fixative mixture to cover the fabric roll.

5. Add enough dye solution to achieve your desired color (½ teaspoon to 2 tablespoons). The more dye, the deeper the color.

6. Zip up the bag and agitate gently to spread the dye. Wash out the dye after 24 hours (see Cleanup, page 93).

Fabric for leaves

DYEING FABRIC FOR PETALS

1. Soak PFD fabric in the fixative mixture for 20 minutes before dyeing. Wring out the fabric. Use premoistened fabric for blurry color transitions or dried fabric for crisp details. (If you want dry fabric, hang it up to dry. Don't put it in the dryer.)

2. Mix the dye solution and fixative mixture to make ½" of dye color in the base of a small, shallow container. Use ½ teaspoon of dye for a pastel color, 2 tablespoons for dark, or any amount that gives the desired strength. Mix several colors of dye in separate containers.

3. Wad fabric and insert it in one container of dye and fixative solution. Re-wad the fabric and insert it in the next container of dye and fixative solution. Repeat as desired.

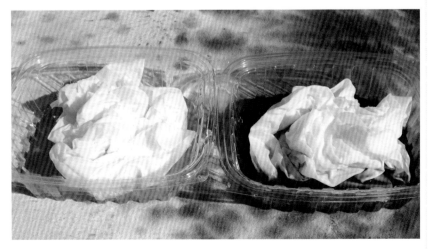

Wadded fabric

4. *Optional*: Mix a diluted dye solution of dye and fixative mixture, by use 1 teaspoon dye to 1 cup fixative or as desired.

5. Pour dye mixture over the fabric in the last container until covered.

6. Wait 1 hour and move fabric to a zip-close bag. Wash after 24 hours (see Cleanup, page 93).

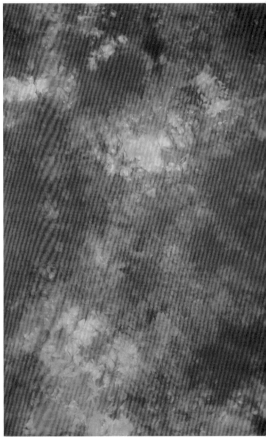

Blotched results

DYEING FABRIC FOR PETALS OR LEAVES

1. Soak fabric in the fixative mixture for 20 minutes. Wring out the fabric.

2. Lay the fabric smooth. Pinch a spot and twist until the fabric piece is twisted tight.

Twisted fabric

3. Place the twisted fabric in a shallow container.

4. Choose several dye colors and dilute them with hot water as desired.

5. Dribble the colors over different areas of the twisted fabric.

Twist fabric in dye solution.

6. Allow to soak for 1 hour and then place in zip-close bag. Wash after 24 hours (see Cleanup, page 93).

Twisted fabric results

DYEING FIREWORKS FABRIC FOR PETALS

1. Soak fabric in the dye fixative mixture for 20 minutes. Wring out the fabric. Allow fabric to dry completely. Start with dry fabric.

2. Always wear a mask, gloves, and old clothing.

3. Fill spray bottle with fixative mixture.

4. Sprinkle a small amount of dye powder onto the completely dry fabric.

5. Spray fabric with fixative and watch the colors move.

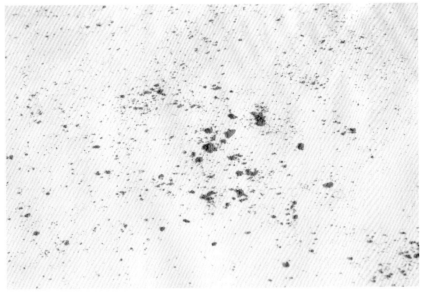

Sprinkle dye powder on dry fabric and spray with fixative.

6. Allow to dry flat. Wash in 24 hours (see Cleanup, at right).

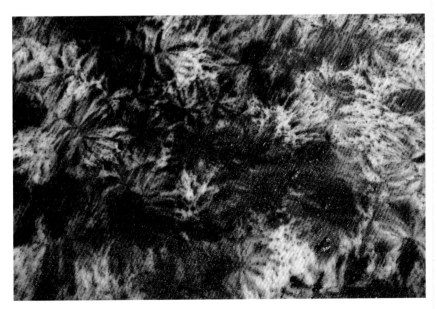

Fireworks fabric

Cleanup

1. Unused dye and fixative mixture may be washed down the drain. Do not pour unused fixative on plants; the salts may be harmful to them.

2. Wash colors separately.

3. Rinse all the excess dye and fixative mixture out of each fabric.

4. Soak dark fabrics in a solution of hot water and 1 teaspoon Retayne dye fixative per yard of fabric.

5. Wash all fabric. Add a Shout Color Catcher sheet and Synthrapol, ¼ cup per washing machine load. Repeat until a Color Catcher sheet comes out clean.

6. Iron fabrics while they are still damp.

Resources

C&T Publishing
Joen Wolfrom's 3-in-1 Color Tool

Whisper Color by Laurel Anderson
www.whispercolor.com
whispercolor@yahoo.com
(916) 531-3163
Patterns, kits, restickable gluestick, bamboo batting

Adobe
www.adobe.com
(800) 585-0774 or (800) 833-6687
Photoshop and Illustrator design software

Big Horn Quilts
www.bighornquilts.com
(877) 586-9150
PFD fabrics, batik fabrics, and batting

Dharma Trading Co.
www.dharmatrading.com
(800) 542-5227
Dyes, chemicals, PFD fabric, fabric paint, and large-sized freezer paper

eQuilter.com
www.equilter.com
(877) 322-7423

Michaels
www.michaels.com
(800) 642-4235
Large sheets of newsprint and tracing paper

Office Depot
www.officedepot.com
(888) 463-3768
Web store for restickable glue and Avery printable fabric sheets

Pixeladies
www.pixeladies.com
(916) 320-8774
Prints photos and words on fabric

PRO Chemical & Dye
www.prochemicalanddye.com
(800) 228-9393
PFD fabrics, dye, and chemicals

Roxanne International
www.thatperfectstitch.com
(800) 993-4445
Glue-Baste-It

Superior Threads
www.superiorthreads.com
(800) 499-1777
King Tut variegated thread, Bottom Line thread, So Fine Thread

About the Author

Laurel Anderson
photo by Teri Fode

Laurel Anderson comes from a long line of fiber artists. They called themselves housewives. Laurel learned to sew, crochet, macramé, tailor, cross-stitch, make stained glass, and tat lace. When her sons started school, she began quilting. She has been quilting long enough to fill four drawers with thread and half the garage with her stash. Pattern design is her favorite part of quilting. When she gets inspired, she makes multiple variations of each idea.

Laurel lives in Carmichael, California, with her husband and three kids. Her website is www.whispercolor.com and she can be reached at WhisperColor@yahoo.com.

Great Titles *from* C&T PUBLISHING

Available at your local retailer or **www.ctpub.com** *or* **800-284-1114**

For a list of other fine books from C&T Publishing, ask for a free catalog:

C&T PUBLISHING, INC.
P.O. Box 1456
Lafayette, CA 94549
800-284-1114

Email: ctinfo@ctpub.com
Website: www.ctpub.com

C&T Publishing's professional photography services are now available to
the public. Visit us at www.ctmediaservices.com.

Tips and Techniques *can be found at www.ctpub.com > Consumer*
Resources > Quiltmaking Basics: Tips & Techniques for Quiltmaking & More

For quilting supplies:

COTTON PATCH
1025 Brown Ave.
Lafayette, CA 94549
Store: 925-284-1177
Mail order: 925-283-7883

Email: CottonPa@aol.com
Website: www.quiltusa.com

Note: Fabrics used in the quilts shown may not be currently
available, as fabric manufacturers keep most fabrics in print for
only a short time.